F I R E P O W E R
AIR WARFARE

FIREPOWER
AIR WARFARE

EDITOR
CHRIS BISHOP

BROWN
BOOKS

ISBN 1-897884-52-4

**Editorial and design by Brown Packaging Books Ltd
Bradley's Close
74-77 White Lion Street
London N1 9PF**

Editor: Chris Bishop

Printed in Singapore

Contents

Introduction

One of the realities for modern military strategists is that whoever commands the air also commands the land and sea. Superiority in the air is often the decisive factor in warfare, a fact first demonstrated by Britain's Royal Air Force during operations against rebellious tribes in the Middle East in the 1930s. There are undoubtedly exceptions to this general rule; perhaps the most obvious is the American experience in Vietnam, where US forces failed in their attempts, despite almost complete air superiority. However, there is also much supporting evidence, most recently in the 1991 Gulf War, that in the majority of circumstances superiority in the air can provide one of two opposing forces with a devastating military advantage.

Air power can broadly be defined as the use of aviation-based weapons systems for military purposes. It has four key aims; firstly, to establish a secure base from which to operate, secondly to obtain air supremacy, thirdly to provide sufficient offensive firepower – through offensive support operations – to enable the army to take the ground, and finally to provide air reconnaissance to establish where to direct the effort, what effect it is having and what the enemy is doing. Modern air forces field specialised units and aircraft and develop tactics which are tailored to achieving these goals. More specifically they aim to fulfil a variety of roles such as attack, air defence, air superiority, maritime patrol and strike, strategic and tactical airlift, reconnaissance, casualty evacuation, search and rescue countermeasures.

This publication takes a detailed look at all aspects of air warfare, often through the eyes and words of those involved, and specifically at military aircraft in past or current use. Such events as, for example, the Falklands air war, are often better told with the benefit of first-hand evidence. Many of the strategies, tactics, individual combats, and aircraft detailed in the book are illustrated, providing the reader with a useful graphic reference.

Left: The F-22 single-seat air superiority fighter will be the replacement for the F-15 Eagle as the USAF's premier air combat fighter.

Originally conceived as an air superiority aircraft, the McDonnell Douglas F-15 Eagle has been successfully adapted into a combat-proven stike platform. The F-15E Strike Eagle aircraft is one of the finest multi-role combat aircraft in the world.

INTERCEPTORS

Interceptors have been around for almost as long as aircraft have gone to war. Speed and the ability to climb fast have always been vital to success, but the pilots trying to deal with Zeppelin attacks in 1916 would not have believed the power and performance available to their successors, less than a lifetime later.

Accelerating under more than 46,000 pounds of thrust, a McDonnell Douglas F-15 Eagle accelerates vertically to high altitude to make an interception.

The classic interception mission, wherein fighters defend territory by attacking huge fleets of enemy bombers, reached a combat peak during World War II. Since then, while interceptors have grown ever more capable, the bomber threat has reduced.

"The flight was controlled by Warton Air Traffic. Visual contact was obtained at about 12 miles and the two aircraft joined at the pre-briefed position to the north of the Mull of Galloway. This allowed both aircraft to fly directly on the supersonic Bravo run at FL330 – 33,000 feet."

It was one of the most realistic interception sorties ever flown by a supersonic fighter, in this case the Tornado F.Mk 2. The target was the one of the few aircraft that could give the fighter a run for its money – Concorde.

Supersonic flight

"Having joined into close formation, the two aircraft were positioned on the supersonic run by Warton ATC and given clearance to accelerate. At 1.2 IMN – Indicated Mach Number – height was increased to 37,000 feet. This speed and height gave the Tornado room to position around Concorde and carry out the photographic mission.

"Both aircraft accelerated to supersonic flight together. The Tornado positioned behind, to the right and left of Concorde. As the fighter came abeam the cockpit of the British Airways SST, the only effect of Mach 1 flight was felt as a little lateral buffeting. This was due to the transition through the major shock wave, or sound barrier.

"Later in the flight, the captain of Concorde noted the same effect as the Tornado flew ahead, although the shock waves were not visible, of course. The supersonic photographic flight was terminated after about 10 minutes, during which the Tornado and Concorde had covered 138 statute miles."

Only on rare occasions were the RAF able to enjoy realistic interceptor training for its Tornado defence force, as the Soviets did not send bombers into Western air-space to train our fighter crews! Surveillance patrols with subsonic Tu-95 'Bear' aircraft were a regular event in the Cold War era, and provided intercept targets for NATO aircraft.

Literally hundreds of 'Bear' flights have been intercepted in recent years, and the Russian crews have long been used to a Lightning, Phantom, Tornado, Tomcat or Eagle escort out of sensitive areas and being shooed off their watch on NATO exercises.

The English Electric Lightning remains one of the fastest climbing interceptors of all time, and with its Firestreak missile armament defended Britain for nearly 30 years.

The fighters photographed the 'Bears' to see if they had any interesting new features such as radar or ECM, inflight-refuelling capability or any visible new weaponry.

Constant alert

The threat has undoubtedly receded, and the emphasis switched to other regions. The Russian Air Force, comprising the Long-Range Aviation, Naval Aviation and air defence units of the former Soviet air force is in the grips of severe financial crisis, but despite the reduction in the size of the fleet the defences are formidable.

The task of aircraft like the S.E.5 and Sopwith Camel was to shoot down German two-seat observation aircraft, spotting for artillery fire and reporting back Allied positions on the ground.

During World War II, interceptors were deployed by all the fighting powers. Right

FLASHBACK

Night hunters

The all-weather interceptor made its first appearance in World War II. After early British experiments, the peak of piston-engined night fighter development came when the Germans were faced with the RAF's massive night bomber campaign in the last two years of the war. The Heinkel He-219 'Uhu' (Owl) displayed all of the attributes of the interceptor fighter, being fast,

The Heinkel He 219 'Uhu' was the most capable night-fighter of World War II.

heavily armed, highly manoeuvrable, and equipped with the most advanced radar and electronic warfare equipment then available. In its first six sorties the first He 219 squadron destroyed no less than 20 Royal Air Force bombers, including six of the previously uncatchable Mosquitoes!

INTERCEPTORS Reference File

159

FRANCE

Dassault-Breguet Mirage III

Although it is now obsolescent in its aerodynamics and powerplant, the classic **Mirage III** remains in widespread service as an interceptor and multi-role warplane. The pre-production Mirage IIIA first flew in May 1958 and established the basic configuration of the series with the 6000-kg (13,228- lb) afterburning thrust Atar 9B turbojet and a low-set delta wing as the core of an aerodynamic platform optimised for the high-altitude interception role.

The first fully operational variant was the **Mirage IIIC** all-weather interceptor, which flew in October 1960 with the Cyrano II radar. There were many other Mirage III variants, then came the radarless Mirage 5 optimised

for the clear-weather attack role. However, the subsequent miniaturisation of electronics has allowed many Mirage 5s to be retrofitted with radar as useful fighters. The Mirage 50 is a Mirage 5 version with the more powerful Atar 9K- 50. The same engine is used in the Mirage 3NG and Mirage 50M variants: both have fixed canard foreplanes, small leading-edge root extensions and other aerodynamic and electronic improvements.

Specification
Dassault-Breguet Mirage 3NG
Type: single-seat all-weather interceptor fighter

Powerplant: one 7200-kg (15,873-lb) afterburning thrust SNECMA Atar 9K-50 turbojet
Performance: maximum speed 2340 km/h (1,454 mph) or Mach 2.2; range not revealed
Dimensions: span 8.22 m (26 ft 11.5 in); length 15.65 m (51 ft 4.25 in)

Weights: empty not revealed; maximum take-off 14700 kg (32,407 lb)
Armament: two 30-mm cannon and up to 4200 kg (9,259 lb) of disposable stores carried externally
User: none built as such, but aircraft of many countries updated to this approximate standard

Above: F-89 Scorpion was the USAF's first all-weather fighter. At the height of the Cold War, America had over 10,000 interceptors for mainland defence. It now has about 2,000.

The Convair F-102 Delta Dagger was introduced in the 1950s. It was armed with the nuclear 'Genie' missile, which exploded in the path of the incoming bombers' armada.

The Professional's View:

Interceptor pilot

"When the call comes in to scramble, you never know what you are going to find. Ground Control gives you a vector, so you can intercept from the stern. That way you can make a nice slow approach, play it cautious. You're here to protect the airspace of the United States, and you have to be ready for anything. Sometimes it will be a civilian pilot in a Cessna, maybe the guy's in trouble. Then you're acting as a kind of aerial Coast Guard, escorting him in to safety. If it's a bad guy, you can divert him out to sea. If he won't go, you can harass him. And if you have to, you kill him. That's what defense is all about."

F-16 pilot, New Jersey Air National Guard

160

SWEDEN

Saab JA 37 Viggen

Sweden's defence posture involves the wartime dispersal of high-performance combat aircraft to any suitable length of road, and this demands STOL field performance with the ability to make no-flare landings at high sink rates. The multi-role type designed to meet these difficult operating conditions in succession to the Saab 35 Draken was the **Viggen** (thunderbolt) with a close-coupled canard layout and a military development of a civil turbofan with a Swedish afterburner and thrust reverser. The type first flew in February 1967 as an attack warplane, and later there appeared the **JA 37** dedicated interceptor using the airframe of the AJ 37 attacker with the vertical tail of the Sk 37 conversion trainer, a more

powerful engine, and electronics and armament optimised for the interception role.

The first of 149 JA 37s entered service in 1979. The electronic core of the variant is the Ericsson UAP-1023 (PS-46/A) radar, which was the first multi-mode pulse-Doppler equipment to enter production anywhere in the world. Though a considerable warload can be carried under the wings, this is generally limited to RB 71 Sky Flash semi-active radar and RB 24/74 Sidewinder IR homing missiles.

Specification
Saab JA 37 Viggen
Type: single-seat all-weather interceptor fighter

Powerplant: one 12750-kg (28,108-lb) afterburning thrust Volvo Flygmotor RM8B (Pratt & Whitney JT8D-22) turbofan
Performance: maximum speed 2125+ km/h (1,320+ mph) or Mach 2+; radius 1000 km (621 miles)
Dimensions: span 10.6 m (34 ft 9.25 in); length 16.4 m (53 ft 9.75 in)
Weights: empty not revealed; maximum take-off 20500 kg (45,194 lb)
Armament: one 30-mm cannon and up to 6000 kg (13,228 lb) of disposable stores carried externally
User: Sweden

RAF Interceptors: Then and Now

Less than 50 years separate the Spitfire and the Tornado, but the performance difference between the two interceptors is phenomenal.

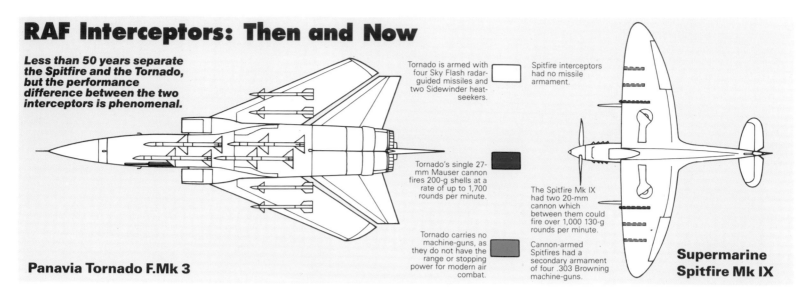

Tornado is armed with four Sky Flash radar-guided missiles and two Sidewinder heat-seekers.

Spitfire interceptors had no missile armament.

Tornado's single 27-mm Mauser cannon fires 200-g shells at a rate of up to 1,700 rounds per minute.

The Spitfire Mk IX had two 20-mm cannon which between them could fire over 1,000 130-g rounds per minute.

Tornado carries no machine-guns, as they do not have the range or stopping power for modern air combat.

Cannon-armed Spitfires had a secondary armament of four .303 Browning machine-guns.

Panavia Tornado F.Mk 3

Supermarine Spitfire Mk IX

---

through the conflict, from the Polish air force desperately trying to stop Luftwaffe bombers over its homeland in 1939 to Japanese fighters equally desperately attempting to prevent US B-29s burning the heart out of their Empire in 1945, the fighter was a force with which to be reckoned.

In between were the bitter combats of the Battle of Britain and the vast air battles over the Third Reich as the Germans sent waves of Fw 190s and Bf 109s against the US B-17s and B-24s by day. At night Bf 110s and Heinkel He 219s exacted a high cost in RAF Lancasters

and Halifaxes systematically bombing industrial and urban targets.

With the war over and the Germans having pointed the way to how future interceptors would look by forming the first jet and rocket squadrons, the Allies rushed to develop new jet fighters of their own. Some had flown before the end of the war, but it was not until 1950 that the Korean War brought the interceptor into action once again.

In Korea, the boot was on the other foot – it was the enemy who made the running in the interceptor stakes when MiG-15s were sent

against B-29 formations. To stop them, the USAF deployed a smaller force of F-86 Sabres, the only high-performance jet type available. Just as in World War II, the bombers usually got through and the interceptors failed to prevent targets being bombed.

Through the late 1950s and early 1960s, jet interceptors became very potent – but the nuclear bomber strike that nations such as Britain, the USA and USSR thought they might one day have to launch, never occurred. Instead, there were 'limited wars'

---

161   UNITED KINGDOM

Panavia Tornado F.Mk 3

The extent of the UK Air Defence Region demands the use of a sizeable force of long-range interceptors whose capabilities are multiplied by the use of airborne early warning aircraft. It was clear from early in the development of the Tornado IDS that this machine could be adapted quite simply into an interceptor to replace the McDonnell Douglas Phantom, and the first prototype of the **Tornado Air-Defence Variant** flew in October 1979 for a service debut in 1986.

The desirability of a semi-recessed installation for the primary armament of Sky Flash missiles resulted in a stretched fuselage, with the spin-off advantages of greater internal fuel capacity and finer lines for reduced

transonic drag. At the same time the nose was revised for the troublesome but potentially excellent Foxhunter radar used with an updated suite of electronics and displays. The first of 180 aircraft entered service as the **Tornado F.Mk 2** with RB199 Mk 103 engines, these machines later being upgraded to **Tornado F.Mk 2A** standard. The definitive version is the **F.Mk 3**.

Specification
Panavia Tornado F.Mk 3
Type: two-seat all-weather interceptor fighter
Powerplant: two 8550-kg (18,849-lb)

afterburning thrust Turbo-Union RB199 Mk 104 turbofans
Performance: maximum speed 2340 km/h (1,454 mph) or Mach 2.2; radius 1853+ km (1,151+ miles)
Dimensions: span 13.91 m (45 ft 7.5 in) spread and 8.6 m (28 ft 2.5 in) swept; length 18.082 m (59 ft 4 in)

Weights: empty 14500 kg (31,966 lb); maximum take-off 27986 kg (61,700 lb)
Armament: one 27-mm cannon and a heavy load of disposable stores
Users: Malaysia, Oman, Saudi Arabia and UK

---

162   FORMER USSR

Mikoyan-Gurevich MiG-25 'Foxbat'

The **MiG-25 'Foxbat'** is the world's fastest combat aeroplane, and was conceived from the late 1950s as a high-altitude interceptor to counter the North American B-70 Valkyrie Mach 3 strategic bomber. The type has a primary structure of nickel steel and titanium, and both field performance and manoeuvrability were sacrificed to maximum climb rate and speed at altitude. Even though the B-70 was cancelled in 1961, the design of the MiG-25 continued to produce a first flight in late 1964 or early 1965.

The basic interceptor has the NATO reporting name **'Foxbat-A'**, and entered service with the IA-PVO (air defence force, 300+ aircraft) and FA (tactical air force, 130+ aircraft) during

1970; the type is partnered by the **MiG-25U 'Foxbat-C'** conversion trainer, which has no radar but a separate cockpit below and forward of the original unit, and two reconnaissance models. The 'Fox Fire' radar of the 'Foxbat-A' is technically obsolescent as it uses valve rather than transistor technology, but this gives the equipment the power to 'burn through' enemy ECM. The radar also provides illumination for the semi-active radar homing version of the huge AA-6 'Acrid' missile.

Specification
Mikoyan-Gurevich MiG-25 'Foxbat-A'
Type: single-seat all-weather

interceptor fighter
Powerplant: two 12250-kg (27,006-lb) afterburning thrust Tumanskii R-31 turbojets
Performance: maximum speed 3400 km/h (2,113 mph) or Mach 3.2; radius 1450 km (901 miles)
Dimensions: span 13.95 m (45 ft

9 in); length 23.82 m (78 ft 1.75 in)
Weights: empty 20000 kg (44,092 lb); maximum take-off 37425 kg (82,507 lb)
Armament: four AA-6 'Acrid' air-to-air missiles carried externally
Users: Algeria, Iraq, Syria and USSR

The Mirage 2000 continues the French tradition of building delta-wing fighters. These have good high-speed, high-altitude manoeuvrability. Mirage 2000s have been sold to air forces around the world.

in Algeria, the Middle East – and Vietnam.

By the 1972 big bomber offensive against Hanoi and Haiphong by SAC B-52s, the nature of war had changed. Then, the North Vietnamese vested their primary defence against bombers in missiles, not their MiG-21 interceptors. It was the SA-2 SAM that caused the losses among the Stratofort cells, very few MiG firing passes being recorded by the bomber crews.

Vietnam changed a lot of thinking about air defence. The threat of nuclear war between the superpowers began to recede as the power of destruction inherent in missiles meant that only total breakdown of diplomacy would lead to war. And in future, the bomber would need stand-off weapons such as cruise missiles if it was to stand any chance of getting through massed ground defences.

But what if there are more conventional, localised wars like Vietnam? Clearly there is

---

163

Sukhoi Su-15 'Flagon'

The **Su-15 'Flagon'** first flew in about 1964 as a development of the Su-11 with genuine Mach 2+ flight performance and equipment suiting the type to operation within the Soviet concept of ground-controlled interception with powerful air launched missiles. Current models are sometimes known in the West under the Su-21 designation.

The oldest variant in service has the NATO reporting name **'Flagon-D'**, and is a development of the 'Flagon-A' with compound-sweep wings of greater span as well as deeper inlets probably indicating the use of more powerful R-13F engines in place of the original R-11F units. Later models are the **'Flagon-E'** introduced in 1973 with a number of improvements including 'Twin Scan' radar and a twin-wheel nose unit for the landing gear; the **'Flagon-F'** definitive single-seater with an ogival rather than conical radome over a more advanced radar providing a limited 'look-down/shoot-down' capability; and the **'Flagon-G'** two-seat conversion and continuation trainer with a second cockpit (complete with periscope) inserted behind the original cockpit. The later models also possess a more flexible armament fit including cannon pods and short-range missiles.

Specification
Sukhoi Su-15 'Flagon-F'
Type: single-seat all-weather interceptor fighter

Powerplant: two 7200-kg (15,873-lb) afterburning thrust Tumanskii R-13F2-300 turbojets
Performance: maximum speed 2655 km/h (1,650 mph) or Mach 2.5; radius 725 km (450 miles)
Dimensions: span 9.15 m (30 ft 0 in); length 21.33 m (70 ft 0 in)

Weights: empty 11000 kg (24,250 lb); maximum take-off 18000 kg (39,683 lb)
Armament: up to four AA-3 'Anab' or AA-8 'Aphid' air-to-air missiles and provision for two 23-mm cannon pods carried externally
User: USSR/former

164

McDonnell Douglas F-4 Phantom II

The **F-4 Phantom II** was designed as a fleet defence fighter and first flew in May 1958. The type was later developed into a land-based interceptor and multi-role warplane for the US Air Force and for export.

Different models were used for interception by Japan, the UK and West Germany. Japan modified 100 of its **140 F-4EJ** fighters to **F-4EJ Kai** standard with APG-66J radar, a head-up display, a laser INS and a more modern radar warning system. The UK operated three Phantom variants in the interception role until 1992.

The Royal Navy received 50 **FGB.MK.1**, with Rolls Royce Spey power; the RAF received 116 **FGR. MK2**, which were upgraded with more capable electronics. West Germany improved 150 of its **F-4F** air-superiority fighters with APG-65 radar and a Litef fire-control system for 'look-down/shoot-down' capability with AIM-120 AMRAAM missiles, as well as a digital databus, a laser INS and a more modern radar-warning system.

The USA now only operates the aircraft in the reconnaissance role, as the **RF-4**, and as the **ECM F-4G 'Wild Weasel.'**

Specification
McDonnell Douglas F-4E Phantom II
Type: two-seat interceptor

Powerplant: two 8119-kg (17,900-lb) afterburning thrust General Electric J79-GE-17A turbojets
Performance: maximum speed 2301 km/h (1,430 mph) or Mach 2.17; radius 1145 km (712 miles)
Dimensions: span 11.77 m (38 ft 7.5 in); length 19.2 m (63 ft 0 in)

Weights: empty 13757 kg (30,328 lb); maximum take-off 28030 kg (61,795 lb)
Armament: one 20-mm multi-barrel cannon and up to 7257 kg (16,000 lb) of disposable stores
Users: Egypt, Greece, Iran, Israel, Japan, South Korea, Turkey, UK, USA and West Germany

The Sukhoi Su-27 'Flanker' is the primary CIS and Ukraine air defence fighter. The example seen here flew to intercept a Royal Norwegian Air Force P-3 Orion maritime reconnaissance aircraft over the Arctic Ocean, in the days when such missions were common.

an even greater need for fighters with human crews to judge if an attack is for real, and make eyeball identification of targets in the way no computerised system is able to do. A fighter pilot can decide not to fire, but a missile, once launched, cannot be turned back.

Missile threat

Thus we have seen some small-scale actions involving interceptor fighters in the years since Vietnam, action that just might have sparked off a wider war if the fast-flying jets had not been around to make on-the-spot judgements, and missiles had been launched instead.

Imagine what might have happened in the Gulf of Sidra in 1981 if the Libyans had fired

surface-to-surface missiles at the US Sixth Fleet rather than make a foolhardy attack on a couple of Tomcats with Su-22s. That skirmish ended in a 2-0 win for the US and the Libyans went home, suitably chastised. A missile strike on American ships could easily have led to something far bigger.

In many future combat scenarios, the manned interceptor will continue to be the primary guardian of national airspace. In Europe the new EFA will take on the role, and the US has the F-117A stealth fighter. The Russians are developing new interceptor fighters for defence as well, so for some time to come, the situation will remain much the same as today.

McDonnell Douglas F-15 'Eagles' from the USAF's 318th Fighter Interceptor Squadron based in Washington State overfly the 14,000-ft peak of Mount Ranier. Although it is a supreme dogfighter, the F-15 can also climb straight and fast and will reach this altitude in less than a minute.

Combat Comparison

The two premier air combat aircraft in the world today are the McDonnell Douglas F-15 Eagle and the Sukhoi Su-27 'Flanker'. Both are large aircraft, heavily armed and with superb performance.

165 USA

McDonnell Douglas F-15 Eagle

Designed from the late 1960s on the basis of early lessons in the Vietnam War, the **F-15 Eagle** first flew in July 1972 and was ordered as the US Air Force's main air-superiority and interceptor fighter in replacement for the McDonnell Douglas F-4 Phantom II and, to a lesser extent, the Convair F-106 Delta Dart. The Soviet fighter that most spurred development of the F-15 was the Mikoyan-Gurevich MiG-25 'Foxbat', but unlike this Soviet type the US fighter possesses an

166 USSR

Sukhoi Su-27 'Flanker'

The **Su-27 'Flanker'** and Mikoyan-Gurevich MiG-29 'Fulcrum' are the two fighters that have brought the USSR to a position of technical parity with the best of Western fighters. The Su-27 is about 30 per cent larger than the MiG-29, and the relationship between the fighters may be regarded as similar to that between their American counterparts, the McDonnell Douglas F-15 Eagle and General Dynamics F-16 Fighting Falcon. The Su-27 is aerodynamically and structurally akin to the F-15 even though it possesses large leading-edge root extensions for increased agility, especially at high angles of attack. The type is more advanced than the MiG-29, and has a fly-by-wire control system, a long-range search and fire-control radar of the pulse-Doppler type that provides a 'look-down/shoot-down' capability with three variants of the AA-10 'Alamo' air-to-air missile and, perhaps most important of all, an IR search and track sensor.

excellent close-combat ability in addition to advanced short/medium-range air-combat capability. The basically conventional airframe is centred on a fuselage supporting widely spaced afterburning turbofans of high power/weight ratio, shoulder-set wings of large area and moderate sweep, and rearward-projecting structural booms for tail surfaces that include horizontal stabilators. In overall terms the airframe is optimised for low drag and sustained manoeuvrability, and also offers a high internal fuel volume. This aerodynamic capability is complemented by advanced electronics (including APG-63 long-range search and fire-control radar) and a cockpit with advanced displays and HOTAS (Hands On Throttle And Stick) controls.

The Eagle entered service in November 1974, and the initial versions were the **F-15A** single-seater and the combat-capable **F-15B** two-seater that was originally designated TF-15A. From 1979 production has been of the much improved **F-15C** and **F-15D** single-

and two-seat versions with provision for external FAST (Fuel And Sensor, Tactical) packs which fit into the angles between the engine trunks and the undersides of the wing to boost fuel capacity by nearly 75 per cent without appreciable drag; the FAST packs also have tangential weapon attachment points allowing an increase in external load from 7258 kg (16,000 lb) to 10705 kg (23,600 lb). The F-15C and F-15D also feature enhanced and more flexible APG-70 radar as well as several other important electronic system improvements.

Specification
McDonnell Douglas F-15C Eagle
Type: single-seat all-weather air-superiority and interceptor fighter
Powerplant: two 10636-kg (23,450-lb) afterburning thrust Pratt & Whitney F100-P-220 turbofans
Performance: maximum speed 2655+ km/h

(1,650+ mph) or Mach 2.5+; range 5745 km (3,570 miles) with FAST packs
Dimensions: span 13.05 m (42 ft 9.75 in); length 19.43 m (63 ft 9 in)
Weights: empty 12973 kg (28,600 lb); maximum take-off 30845 kg (68,000 lb)
Armament: one 20-mm multi-barrel cannon and up to 10705 kg (23,600 lb) of disposable stores carried externally
Users: Israel, Japan, Saudi Arabia and USA

The F-15 established several performance records during development. In addition to being very agile, it is one of the fastest fighters around, and has superb climbing ability. It is also possessed of very long range, a vital characteristic in these days when attackers can use stand-off weapons.

The F-15 pilot's bubble canopy gives superb all-round visibility. As the aircraft was designed in the 1960s and 1970s, the cockpit itself is old-fashioned, having none of the latest electronic displays and controls.

Standard weapon fit on the F-15 is four short-range heat-seeking missiles, four radar-homing medium range missiles, and a gun. The Israelis have used the F-15 in combat, and rarely use the medium-range missiles.

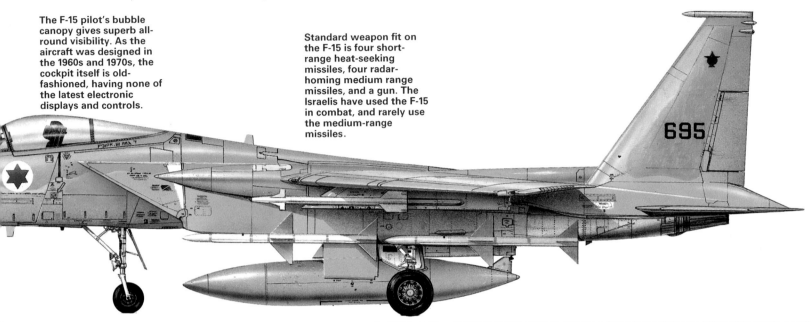

The Su-27 first flew during 1977 in its 'Flanker-A' pre-production form with curved wingtips and its twin vertical tail surfaces located centrally above the engine jetpipes. The variant that entered service with the IA-PVO (air defence force) in 1986 is the 'Flanker-B' with leading edge flaps, revised square-cut wingtips with missile rails, and the vertical tail surfaces moved out onto the tailplane booms. The 'Flanker-C' two seat model has a full capability nose. Two seat version for training was designated SU-27UB. Carrier version SU-27K was abandoned. SU-27PU two-seat long-range interceptor. SU-30M is a related aircraft for ground attack. SU-35 is the most advanced model currently offered.

Specification
Sukhoi Su-27 'Flanker-B'
Type: single-seat counter-air and interceptor fighter
Powerplant: two 13600-kg (29,982-lb) afterburning thrust Lyul'ka AL-31F turbofans
Performance: maximum speed 2495 km/h (1,550 mph) or Mach 2.35; radius 1500 km (932 miles)
Dimensions: span 14.7 m (48 ft 2.75 in); length 21.9 m (71 ft 10.2 in)

Weights: empty 17700 kg (39,021 lb); maximum take-off 30000 kg (66,138 lb)
Armament: one 30-mm multi-barrel cannon and up to about 6000 kg (13,228 lb) of disposable stores carried externally
User: Russian Fed and Ukraine

Probably a little slower than the F-15, the 'Flanker' is even more manoeuvrable. It is as good as, if not better than, its Western equivalents.

The latest generation of Soviet fighters have much improved pilot visibility, but their cockpits are less advanced than the latest Western examples.

'Flanker' is heavily armed, with short- and medium-range versions of the latest AA-10 'Alamo' missile being carried in both heat-seeking and radar-guided variants.

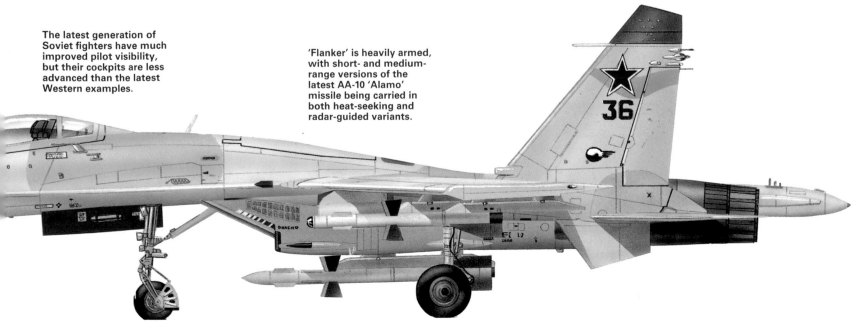

massive raids on the heart of the Reich, opposed in their turn by swarms of German fighters. The Luftwaffe was unable to stop the bombing, but it inflicted heavy losses on the Allies. The bombing campaign had less effect on German industrial production and morale than had been expected. The only successful strategic campaign of the war was mounted by the Americans in the Pacific, with fleets of B-29 Superfortresses tearing the heart out of the Japanese heartland, flying at speeds and heights beyond the reach of most Japanese interceptor fighters.

Above: Ground crew check a squadron of Focke-Wulf Fw 190 fighters. In 1943, German pilots found themselves in the same situation as their British counterparts of 1940, waiting on the ground for a scramble to meet the marauding bombers high above.

Above: A Boeing B-17 Flying Fortress falls in blazing ruin after being hit over Germany in 1944. German fighters wreaked fearful havoc among the heavy bombers, and it was not until the development of American escort fighters that they could penetrate the skies over the Third Reich with any safety.

Above: The Lockheed P-80 Shooting Star was America's first operational jet. A two-seat radar-equipped variant, the F-94, was one of the first all-weather jet interceptors. The Starfire was armed with machine-guns and unguided rockets, but the pace of 1950s aircraft development made it quickly obsolete.

Above: The former Soviet Union and now the Russian Federation has long borders to defend. The massive American nuclear bomber force of the 1950s posed the Soviets a problem. As a result, they developed large, long-ranged fighters such as the Tupolev Tu-128, which were armed with huge air-to-air missiles.

Left: Almost the exact opposite of the huge Tupolev design, the Lockheed F-104 Starfighter was little more than a manned missile. Fast, and with a phenomenal rate of climb, it was a classic Cold War interceptor.

ary fuel

can carry or 2250- on each of s. The lly to stay n of flight ranges. tanks the early

18

Naviga

The twin-
high work
long-range
interceptio
tasks are
navigator
planning,
of targets
Flash mis
fly the air
the close-

A formation of McDonnell Douglas F-15 fighters head into the stratosphere. While most targets now fly at low level, modern fighter radars allow the interceptor to engage them from high above, where performance is at its most economical and the fighter has maximum radar intercept range.

THE MODERN INTERCEPTOR

The threat

The development of high-performance, long-range radars and of effective surface-to-air missiles meant that the day of the high-flying bomber was over. Now, if a bomber wants to penetrate enemy airspace, it has to fly fast and low, beneath the radar coverage. This increases fuel consumption considerably, and would normally decrease combat range, but the introduction of inflight-refuelling has extended those combat ranges indefinitely. A greater threat has come from the increasing capability of offensive weapons. To make an old-style free-fall bomb-run it is necessary for an aircraft to fly right up to a target. By contrast, with stand-off missiles a bomber can attack from tens, or hundreds, or even thousands of kilometres' distance. To make effective interceptions, the defending fighter has to hunt down a fast-moving target flying a few feet above the ground, and it must get to that target before it can launch its missiles.

Above: The main airborne threat today comes from missiles. The AS-4 'Kitchen' was the first modern Soviet threat, capable of more than three times the speed of sound and with a range of nearly 500 kilometres.

Left: Interceptors are often called to identify strange radar contacts. Often these are harmless, but occasionally a scramble will meet a Soviet snooper like this 'Bear', probing at the West's defences.

Weapons

The first interceptors were armed with machine-guns and cannon, and had to get to within a few hundred metres of a target to knock it down. The latest interceptors have powerful and sophisticated radars that can fix multiple targets at great distances. Their primary armament is the radar-guided missile, effective at ranges from 50 to 140 kilometres or more. For close-in fighting and self-protection they also carry short-range heat-seeking dogfight missiles, as well as a powerful, fast-firing gun.

Below: Currently the most capable defender of the Russian Federation, the Sukhoi Su-27 'Flanker' is armed with AA-10 'Alamo missiles. These have ranges of 30 kilometres (in the radar-guided variant) and five kilometres (in the infra-red homing version).

Above: Matra has developed the high-performance Super 530 missile for the French air force. With a range of 25 kilometres, it can engage targets flying 7000 metres higher or lower than the launching aircraft .

Right: In the early days of air-to-air missiles, when accuracy could not be relied upon, the USAF deployed the Douglas AIR-2A Genie. This nuclear-tipped weapon was probably the most fearsome air-to-air missile ever devised.

Detection and control

The performance and range of modern bombers and their weapon means that they have to be detected and intercepted at as great a range as possible. Ground-based radars are powerful, but it is almost impossible for them to detect a low-flying target beyond the horizon. The simplest solution is to extend that horizon, by increasing the height of the radar. Practical airborne early warning appeared at the end of World War II, and the systems are now highly sophisticated. But AEW aircraft are more than flying radar stations, although their primary function is to detect incoming targets at ranges of hundreds of kilometres. They are also fitted with comprehensive command and control systems. Operating closely with patrolling interceptors, they can direct those fighters to deal with an enemy at the first possible moment.

Right: A systems operator aboard an E-3 AWACs airborne early warning aircraft checks air traffic over a large part of the western United States.

Left: Air defence is a complex task, interweaving the reports from massive land-based radar systems with airborne radar information and with other sources of intelligence

Above: Boeing's E-3 AWACS is more than a flying radar station. It has all the communications gear necessary to detect targets and control defending fighters over areas of tens of thousands of square miles.

Right: Although not strictly designed for the purpose, lacking as it does the long-range radar and missiles of larger interceptors, the General Dynamics F-16 Fighting Falcon is a vital component in the defence of the United States.

Far right: Seen climbing vertically over the Alps, the Mirage 2000 makes a fine interceptor. Its RDI radar is designed to pick up an aircraft-sized target at ranges of 100 kilometres or more.

An East German MiG-21 interceptor makes a rocket assisted take-off. Radical changes in Europe signalled the end of such classic Cold War interceptors, but for as long as man uses violence or the threat of violence to solve his differences, there will be warplanes.

Performance

The classic interceptor had to get into action at very short notice. High speed and a superb rate of climb were essential. Fighters like the English Electric Lightning could travel at twice the speed of sound and climb at 50,000 feet per minute. With the scene of the action shifting hundreds of miles from defended coastlines, such performance is not enough. Interceptors are expected to patrol for hours, hundreds of miles from home. Long range and economical fuel consumption are essential, although inflight-refuelling helps extend endurance. The interceptor should also have good trans-sonic acceleration, and be able to deal with targets at all altitudes.

The Shootdown of KE007

As the Korean airliner KE007 made its way home to Seoul, Soviet air defences along the Pacific were on alert. Their airspace had been intruded upon, and they were under instructions to intercept and destroy the trespassing aircraft.

At 0326 (local time) on the morning of 1 September 1983, Major Vassily Kasmin, an experienced Soviet fighter pilot, launched two deadly AA-3 'Anab' air-to-air missiles from the underwing pylons of his Sukhoi Su-21 'Flagon-E' interceptor. Seconds later the radar homing missile tore into the fuselage of a Korean Airlines Boeing 747 Jumbo Jet, while the infra-red homing missile smashed into an engine. A Japanese squid fisherman in the area later reported that "a violent explosion shook the air and a brilliant orange flash lit the south-eastern sky. The light flared for several seconds, succeeded by a round of fireworks and another, less powerful, explosion. After five minutes the smell of burning fuel wafted over the boat".

The Boeing was carrying 29 crew and 240 passengers on a scheduled flight from Anchorage airport, in Alaska, to Seoul, South Korea. The airliner was some 300 miles north-west of its intended route, and had just flown over two of the most sensitive military areas in the world, first the Kamchatka Peninsula, packed with SAM sites, ICBM sites, airfields and a major nuclear submarine base, and then over the Island of Sakhalin, home to a number of important military bases. Ever since, the story of what really happened to Korean Airlines Flight KE007 has been

the subject of great interest, much speculation, and a string of legal actions, with a host of incredible and completely unproven theories being circulated in some quarters. If these are stripped away, one is left with a mystery equal to that surrounding the *Marie Celeste*.

Anchorage leg

Flight KE007, a Boeing 747-200 of Korean Airlines, began its journey to disaster at 0405 GMT, when it lifted off from New York on the first leg of its long journey to Seoul, South Korea. It arrived at Anchorage at 1130 GMT, where it was refuelled, a new flight crew took over and a few passengers got off the aircraft to stretch their legs.

The new flight crew were all extremely experienced on the Boeing 747. The Captain, Chun Byung In, an ex-Korean air force fighter pilot, had a total of 10,600 hours, 6,618 of them on the

Boeing 747. He had a reputation for thoroughness and had been selected to be the President's personal pilot. The co-pilot, Son Dung Hui, was another ex-military pilot, with some 9,000 flying hours, 3,441 on the 747. The flight engineer, Kim Eui Dong, also had a military background, and 2,614 of his 4,000 flying hours had been amassed on the 747.

It is difficult to imagine that these three experienced aircrew could have erred in programming the aircraft's complex triple Inertial Navigation Systems. No-one knows what actually happened on the flight deck before the fateful take-off, but if normal procedures had been followed, engineer Kim or co-pilot Son would have inserted the co-ordinates of the runway and of the waypoints along the route into the computer. He could have punched these in by hand, but it seems more likely that he would have used a pre-prepared cassette supplied by Continental Airlines.

Airway warning

Navigation on this leg of the route would have been closely monitored, since the airway 'Romeo 20' which they would be using passed very close to Soviet airspace, prominently marked on the maps with the legend 'Warning: aircraft infringing upon non-free flying territory may be fired upon without warning'. The crew would have been aware of Soviet sensitivity to any intrusions of this important strategic area, and that, because of frequent sorties by USAF RC-135 reconnaissance aircraft, Soviet defences would be alert to any aircraft straying from the airway.

Soviet Sukhoi Su-15 'Flagon' interceptors streak towards their target. They are huge aircraft, with long combat radius, and long-range radar – essential for patrolling the enormous Soviet borders.

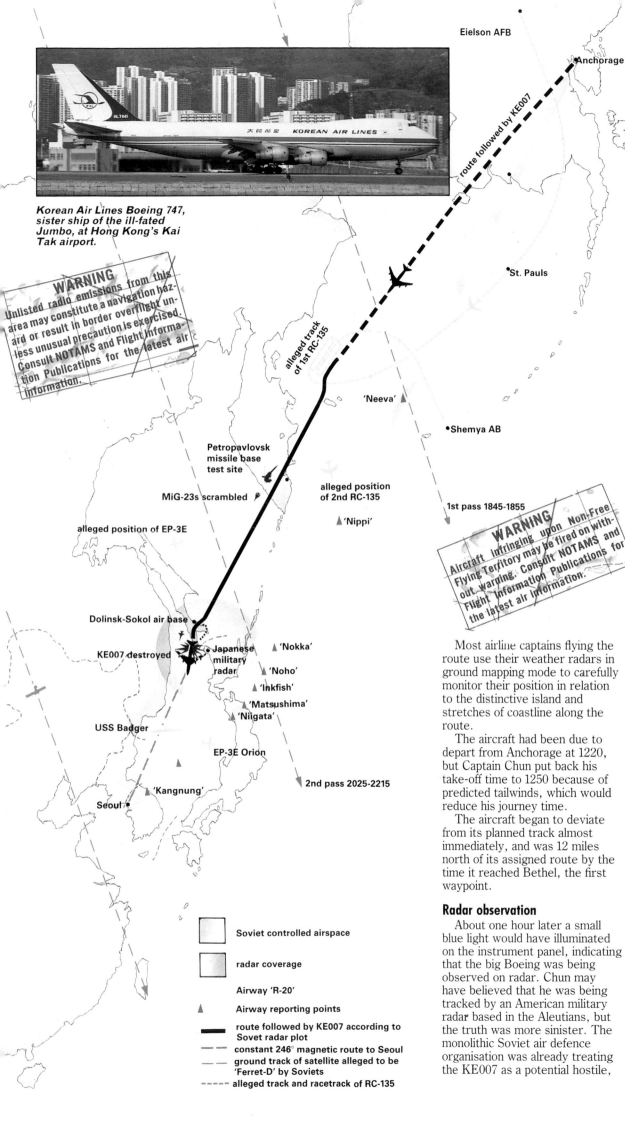

Korean Air Lines Boeing 747, sister ship of the ill-fated Jumbo, at Hong Kong's Kai Tak airport.

The events surrounding the shootdown of the Korean Air Lines Boeing 747 have been subject to much controversy. This map shows the flight path of the aircraft, intended flight path and the defences and US reconnaissance assets operating in the area during the time of the airspace incursions. Apparently the cause of most confusion was the Boeing RC-135 operating from Eielson in Alaska and returning to Shemya in the Aleutians.

initially referring to the radar blip as an RC-135, and later simply as 'the target'.

At 1435 Captain Chun discovered that he was unable to pass a position report to Anchorage. His radio call was heard and relayed by another Korean Airlines aircraft.

At 1600 the other KAL aircraft relayed a message that KE007 was passing the Neeva waypoint. In fact the straying Jumbo was 150 miles further north, about to enter Soviet airspace, and heading straight for the Kamchatka Peninsula 400 miles ahead. Moments later a USAF RC-135 electronic intelligence-gathering aircraft crossed in front of the Korean aircraft, leading to later claims by the Russians that there had been a deliberate rendezvous.

Fighters scrambled

As the Boeing flew over the Kamchatka Peninsula six Soviet MiG-23 'Flogger' fighters were apparently scrambled, but not until the last moment, and they apparently failed to intercept the aircraft. As they crossed the west coast the co-pilot made a radio call, reporting that they were passing waypoint Nippi. By this time they were 250 miles further north. Less than an hour ahead lay the island of Sakhalin, where Soviet fighters were already being prepared to intercept the intruder.

At 1742 GMT, the Soviet fighter controllers scrambled a further four interceptors, flown by the most senior and experienced pilots from the squadrons based at Dolinsk Sokol airbase. The pilots must have been tense and keyed up; they were aware that the intruder had already managed to evade their colleagues over Kamchatka, and they knew that they must not fail. The first aircraft to blast into the inky blackness was a Sukhoi Su-21 'Flagon-F', flown by Major Vassily Kasmin. It was followed into the air by three MiG-23 'Floggers'. The vivid glow from their afterburners was soon swallowed up as the formation climbed arrow-like into the low clouds.

Most airline captains flying the route use their weather radars in ground mapping mode to carefully monitor their position in relation to the distinctive island and stretches of coastline along the route.

The aircraft had been due to depart from Anchorage at 1220, but Captain Chun put back his take-off time to 1250 because of predicted tailwinds, which would reduce his journey time.

The aircraft began to deviate from its planned track almost immediately, and was 12 miles north of its assigned route by the time it reached Bethel, the first waypoint.

Radar observation

About one hour later a small blue light would have illuminated on the instrument panel, indicating that the big Boeing was being observed on radar. Chun may have believed that he was being tracked by an American military radar based in the Aleutians, but the truth was more sinister. The monolithic Soviet air defence organisation was already treating the KE007 as a potential hostile,

Above: The Su-15 had a large, powerful radar in its nose, and relied on huge ground radars to guide it onto its victim. The aircraft has been retired from service.

Left: As the Korean Air Lines Boeing 747 continues on its way, the Soviet interceptor fires two 'Anab' missiles. One missile is heat-seeking and the other radar-controlled.

Left: Once the airliner had been shot down, aircraft from America such as this Orion soon joined in the search for wreckage.

"The target is destroyed..."

Shortly after the destruction of KE007, the Soviets released a transcript of the radio exchanges during the intercept. It provides a clear and dramatic insight into the deadly mission.

1805:05 Su-21 Callsign 805
805, on heading 240.

1805:56 Su-21 Callsign 805
Am observing.

1806:00 Su-21 Callsign 805
Roger. I'm flying behind.

The Soviet fighter is flying behind the airliner, on the same heading, closing slowly. Interceptors approach from astern.

1807:50 Su-21 Callsign 805
Remainder three tonnes.

The Soviet pilot reports his fuel state, obviously in response to a query by his ground control station. Like most 1960s vintage fighters the Su-21 'Flagon-F' is thirsty, so his endurance is very limited.

Su-21 Callsign 805
To the left, surely. Not to the right.

1808:06 Su-21 Callsign 805
Am executing heading 260.

After receiving an order from the ground the pilot alters course to fly off to starboard, away from the airliner. The pilot of the interceptor should position himself on the port side of the target, at the same height, no closer than 1,000 ft away.

Su-21 Callsign 805
On heading 260 . . . Roger.

1808:31 Su-21 Callsign 805
Should I turn off the system? . . . Roger.

1809:00 Su-21 Callsign 805
Affirmative, it has turned

. . . The target is 80, to my left.

1809:35 Su-21 Callsign 805
Executing 240.

The Soviet pilot turns back onto his original heading to fly along parallel to the port side of the 747.

1810:16 Su-21 Callsign 805
Executing 220.

1810:35 Su-21 Callsign 805
But heading is 220.

The Soviet pilot flies back towards the airliner, possibly taking up position in front of the 747. In a Soviet television interview the pilot later claimed, ''as I approached the plane I flashed my navigation lights. Naturally there is a large crew on such an aircraft and they must have seen my flashing lights . . . And then I waggled my wings. He must have seen me. This signified 'you're an intruder', he had to answer 'yes, I'm an intruding aircraft but I'm in trouble' and I would have helped him'. . . he could have landed at our airfield and we would have sorted it out.''

1810:51 Su-21 Callsign 805
Roger. Target is flying with strobe light.

1811:20 Su-21 Callsign 805
8,000 . . .

The Soviet pilot descends to 8,000 metres, taking him below the airliner.

1811:25 Su-21 Callsign 805
Am observing it visually und see it on the screen

1812:15 Su-21 Callsign 805

Roger.

1813:05 Su-21 Callsign 805
I see it. I'm locked onto the target.

1813:26 Su-21 Callsign 805
The target isn't responding to the call.

The Soviet Union claimed that the pilot of '805' attempted to contact Flight 007 on the international distress frequency of 121.5MHz.

1813:35 Su-21 Callsign 805
Affirmative. The target's heading is 240 degrees.

1813:40 Su-21 Callsign 805
Switched on.

1814:10 Su-21 Callsign 805
Roger. It's on the previous one for now.

1814:34 Su-21 Callsign 805
Roger. I have speed. I don't need to turn on my afterburner.

1814:41 Su-21 Callsign 805
My remainder is 2,700.

1818:34 Su-21 Callsign 805
The air navigation lights are on. The strobe light is on.

The Soviet fighter has again approached Flight 007, and the pilot reports his observations to his controller.

1818:56 MiG-23 Callsign 163
Roger, I'm at 7 and a half. Heading 230.

The second Soviet fighter reports his height as 7,500 metres. He is climbing rapidly to join the chase.

Below: Soviet spyships were soon on the scene of the disaster, trying to prevent the Americans finding the evidence first.

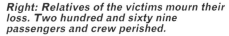

Above: Some examples of another standard Soviet interceptor, the MiG-23 'Flogger-B', also chased the Korean airliner, but they were unable to catch it.

Left: Flying low over American warships, this Soviet maritime reconnaissance Il-18 'May' keeps an eye on the search activity.

Right: Relatives of the victims mourn their loss. Two hundred and sixty nine passengers and crew perished.

Left: Wearing the colours of the Russian airline Aeroflot, this 'passenger' aircraft was in fact a reconnaissance plane in disguise, spying on the American task force.

1819:02 Su-21 Callsign 805

I am closing on the target.

1819:08 Su-21 Callsign 805

There will be enough time.

The pilot of '805' has obviously been asked whether he can do something within a certain time, probably make another attempt to contact the Boeing before it leaves Soviet airspace.

1819:44 MiG-23 Callsign 163

I am flying behind the target at a distance of 25.

The second Soviet interceptor is closing fast, and is already only 25 km behind the airliner.

1820:08 Su-21 Callsign 805

Fiddlesticks! That is, my ZG is already on.

The Soviet fighter pilot reports that he is already locked on to the target.

1820:08 Tokyo ATG

Korean Air Zero Zero Seven, clearance. Tokyo ATC clears Korean Air Zero Zero Seven to climb to and maintain Flight Level 350.

Tokyo clears Flight 007 to climb to a new cruising altitude of 35,000 feet.

1820:20 KE007

Roger, Korean Air Zero Zero Seven, climb maintain 350, leaving 330 this time.

Flight 007 acknowledges its climb clearance and reports that it is already leaving its previous cruising height of 33,000 ft.

1820:30 Su-21 Callsign 805

I am firing cannon bursts.

The Soviet pilot later stated that he fired four bursts of tracer shells 'right by his nose. They can be seen by night for many kilometres, and this was right next to him' as the Korean airliner nears the coast the Soviet pilots are running out of time and options.

1820:30 Tokyo ATC

Tokyo, Roger.

As the Soviet pilot fires his four bursts of tracer Tokyo ATC acknowledges Flight 007's transmission.

1821:24 Su-21 Callsign 805

Yes, I'm approaching the target. I'm going in closer.

1821:35 Su-21 Callsign 805

The target has a strobe light. I have already approached the target, at a distance of about two kilometres.

1821:40 Su-21 Callsign 805

The target is flying at 10,000.

1821:51 MiG-23 Callsign 163

I see both. Distance 10 to 15 kilometres.

1822:02 Su-21 Callsign 805

The target is reducing speed.

1822:23 Su-21 Callsign 805

Increased speed.

1822:29 Su-21 Callsign 805

Negative. It is decreasing speed.

1822:42 Su-21 Callsign 805

You should have . . . earlier. I'm already AG abeam of the target.

1822:55 Su-21 Callsign 805

Not much now. I have to fall back a bit from the target.

1823:05 Su-21 Callsign 805

Say again.

The Soviet pilot is surprised by the airliner's sudden climb, which he interprets as a reduction in airspeed. It catches him unawares, and he snaps at his controller as he struggles to avoid overtaking his target.

1823:08 Tokyo ATC

Korean Air Zero Zero Seven, Tokyo, Roger.

The crew of Flight 007 report that they are level at 35,000 feet.

1823:10 Su-21 Callsign 805

The target's altitude is 10,000.

1823:18 Su-21 Callsign 805

From me AG it is now located 70 to the left.

1823:37 Su-21 Callsign 805

I'm already dropping back. Now I will try a rocket.

1823:49 MiG-23 Callsign 163

12 to the target. I see both.

1825:11 Su-21 Callsign 805

I am closing on the target, am in lock-on. Distance to target 8.

1825:16 Su-21 Callsign 805

I have already switched on.

1825:46 Su-21 Callsign 805

ZG.

With this terse code word the pilot reports that his missiles are locked on.

1826:20 Su-21 Callsign 805

I have executed the launch.

1826:22 Su-21 Callsign 805

The target is destroyed.

1826:27 Su-21 Callsign 805

I am breaking off the attack.

1827:00 KE007

All Engines . . . Rapid decompression . . . One Zero One . . . two Delta . . .

This last transmission from Flight 007 was garbled and difficult to hear on the air traffic control transcripts.

DEFENCE OF THE REALM

Britain's air defences depend on intercepting enemy bombers a long way out before they launch their stand-off nuclear missiles. That responsibility rests with the Tornado F.Mk 3.

Ever since Britain was saved by the pilots of Fighter Command in the Battle of Britain, it has been clear that the air defences of the United Kingdom were vitally important to the survival of the nation. In the Cold War years now coming to an end, Britain was a prime Warsaw Pact target, being NATO's vital rear depot and collecting point for men and supplies, as well as being the base for a third of the Alliance's combat aircraft. As a result, the RAF's responsibility was both to protect the citizens of the United Kingdom and to keep NATO's supply lines open.

The UK Air Defence Region covers nearly 10½ million square kilometres (four million square miles) around Britain's coasts, from the Channel and the North Sea round via the Shetlands and Faeroes out into the Atlantic almost as far as Iceland. Such a huge area re-

quires continual vigilance to patrol.

Vigilance is not enough in the modern world of fast, cruise missile-armed, low flying bombers. During the 1980s, Britain upgraded her defences to cope with the new threat. It had been a far-reaching programme involving the introduction of the Tornado F.Mk 3 interceptor; the Boeing E-3 AWACS aircraft (in the role originally intended for the ill-fated Nimrod AEW); completely new mobile ground radars; new command and control centres hardened against nuclear attack; expanded missile defences; increased weapons stocks; increasing the number of interceptors available by arming Hawk trainers with AIM-9 Sidewinders; and developing a highly computerised nationwide command and communications network to improve battle management.

Below: Tornado has exceptional range, but still needs to be refuelled in the air to carry out its long-distance patrols. The interceptor is just one member of the team, which also includes tankers, control aircraft and shorter-range fighters.

Sporting four large longer-ranged Sky Flash and two Sidewinder missiles, the Tornado makes a potent weapons platform. But for close-in work it also has a 27-mm Mauser cannon.

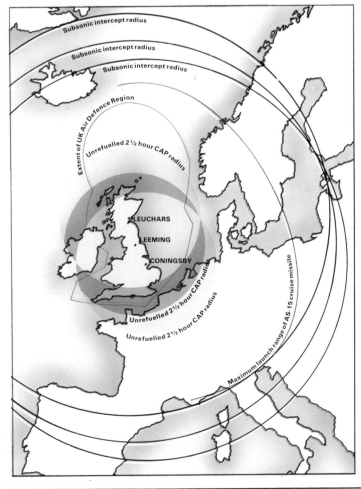

Above and left: Tornados will be controlled by Boeing E-3A AWACS aircraft, which patrol for long periods hundreds of miles out over the sea, tracking enemy bombers.

Detection

Britain's original Battle of Britain radar network was concentrated on the east coast, in face of the threat from the Continent. The threat from the Soviet Union's long-range missile-armed aircraft can come from any direction, and the radar coverage has been extended to cover the Atlantic 'back door'. Ground-based radars are powerful and sophisticated devices, able to detect and track targets out to ranges of 650 kilometres (400 miles). These are augmented by air-borne radar. Until 1990 this capability was limited, provided as it was by ancient Shackleton aircraft, but is now the task of the RAF's Boeing E-3 AWACS. These sophisticated aircraft have doubled the detection range of the nation's air defences, with the added advantage that they can detect low-level, sea-skimming targets.

 **Alert**

Any unidentified airborne target detected approaching United Kingdom airspace has to be investigated. In peacetime, the RAF maintains pairs of fighters on QRA (quick reaction alert) on RAF stations at Leuchars, Leeming and Coningsby. These can be 'scrambled' within minutes to intercept and identify the incoming aircraft. Climbing rapidly, a Tornado will transit to the target area at high level to conserve fuel. It will be vectored onto the target by a controller. In the 1980s the target was invariably a Soviet Tu-95 'Bear' pecking at Britain's defences and checking on reaction times. These giant machines are visible from miles away, and have a huge radar cross-section. However, their regular missions allowed the RAF to practise intercepts against the real thing, and show the Soviets that Britain's defences were effective.

Long range interception

The prime threat to British air space is Soviet missile-launching bombers that can launch their cruise missiles from hundreds of kilometres out. Because the low-flying missiles themselves are difficult to detect and shoot down, it's important that the bomber is destroyed before it launches its weapons. This means that Tornado must be able to operate as far out as Norway.

It would be impossible for the Tornado to scramble from its base and intercept an enemy bomber this far out so, instead, the aircraft flies a combat patrol pattern around the likely bomber routes. Not far away will be the tanker and AWACS control aircraft.

Left: This diagram shows the three Tornado fighter bases and the extent of its patrol areas. The patrol areas can be extended by inflight-refuelling and flying subsonically rather than supersonically.

Above: A Panavia Tornado of the German Luftwaffe makes a low-level pass along the English Channel. Manufactured by a tri-national consortium, the Tornado is one of the fastest aircraft in the world at low level. This is a great advantage in the strike mission – where flying at high speed, inches off the ground, is of vital importance.

FLASHBACK

Ground crew check out an early Typhoon of No. 175 Squadron as armourers wheel up a pair of 500-lb bombs. Typhoons used bombs, rockets and cannon against a wide variety of targets from 1943 to 1945.

The Typhoon

Originally designed as an interceptor, the Typhoon was nearly cancelled, but was saved from oblivion by re-assignment as a ground attack fighter-bomber. It had been intended as a replacement for the Spitfire, but was a cruel disappointment to the RAF. Flying faster from ground level to 10,000 feet, the Typhoon lost most of its power at the altitude where most air combat took place. This was an insurmountable setback, for even with its supercharger, the huge 2,200-hp engine could not compensate for the seven tons it had to move through the sky — against a mere 3.5 tons for the Spitfire. However, at low level the Typhoon's performance was breathtaking, and it was the first RAF fighter to be capable of 400 mph. Some Typhoon pilots were able to score kills against enemy fighters, and countering attacks by Focke-Wulf Fw 190 hit-and-run raiders was an early Typhoon task. The Typhoon was a wonderful war machine, with its formidable armament of four 20-mm cannon and two 1,000-lb bombs or eight 60-lb rockets.

spasms of fire and noise, severing the enemy artillery convoy. Tracers flash in the night but, again, it is too late for gunfire to halt the Tornados – now back at treetop level, speeding back towards friendly lines. The enemy has been dealt a stunning blow by strike aircraft.

The interdiction mission

Strike aircraft are those heavily-burdened fighter-bombers and attack planes that bring bombs, missiles, and sometimes gunfire, both against an enemy at the front *and* many miles behind the actual fighting. They're responsible for interdiction: preventing the flow of enemy men and equipment from reaching the battle area.

Some strike aircraft began life as fighters.

STRIKE AIRCRAFT Reference File

339
GERMANY/ITALY/UNITED KINGDOM

Panavia Tornado IDS

The backbone of Britain's strike capability since January 1982, when No. 9 Squadron took delivery of its first aircraft, the **Tornado** was also the RAF's first variable-geometry aircraft.

The initial production aircraft were all designed to have IDS (interdiction/strike) capability, using a wide variety of NATO weaponry. The Tornado entered service with the German Luftwaffe and Marineflieger in 1982, and the Italian air force received its first examples in the same year. As with most current types designed for ground attack, the Tornado has a useful built-in armament of two Mauser cannon and can deliver all types of ordnance, from small conventional practice bombs to nuclear weapons.

Currently equipping 10 RAF squadrons as the **Tornado GR 1**, the type is reckoned to be among the world's best for low-level, 'under the radar' strikes, its sophisticated avionics enabling it to carry out a terrain-hugging attack with Paveway laser-guided bombs or anti-radiation missiles, such as ALARM. In the battlefield support role, Tornados would be able to deliver such weapons as BL 755 cluster bombs and JP233 runway denial munitions as well as HE bombs.

Specification
Panavia Tornado IDS (RAF GR 1)
Type: two-seat interdiction/strike aircraft

Powerplant: two 7258-kg (16,000-lb) Turbo-Union RB 199 Mk 103 augmented turbofans
Performance: maximum speed Mach 2.2 (2337 km/h) at 11000 m (36,000 ft); service ceiling 15240 m (50,000 ft); range 1390 km (863 miles)
Dimensions: span spread 13.9 m

(45 ft 7 in); swept 8.6 m (28 ft 2 in)
Weights: empty 14091 kg (31,065 lb); loaded 27200 kg (60,000 lb)
Armament: two 27-mm Mauser cannon, plus up to 8156 kg (18,000 lb) of external stores
Users: Germany, Italy, Saudi Arabia and UK

Four bombed-up F-15E Eagles set off on a sortie. Developed from the F-15 air superiority fighter, the 'E' model is crammed with new electronics that enable the big fighter to make pinpoint attacks, whatever the weather and visibility.

Others were conceived for the strike mission. The American F-111, though labelled with an 'F' for 'fighter', was never intended for dogfighting. It is a strike aircraft only.

Few modern weapons of war are more devastating. In the 1990s, strike aircraft can carry precision-guided bombs that are steered onto their targets by lasers or hi-tech electro-optical systems, air-to-ground missiles directed by radar or television, and gravity bombs using new chemical mixes to create a huge explosive force. Some of these 'things under wings' are as mean-spirited as a weapon can be – like the BL 755 ('bomb live'), a canister that can spray enemy personnel with 147 miniscule bomblets.

Many modern strike aircraft must do their job at night or in bad weather. A typical strike aircraft uses terrain-following radar to approach its target at low level (where detection by the enemy is difficult), FLIR (forward-looking infra-red) to locate and identify the target, and computerised 'black boxes' to aim bombs or rockets where they will inflict the most damage.

The job carried out by strike aircraft is sometimes derided as the 'mud-moving' mission because an exploding bomb – at least if it misses – re-arranges the ground in violent, heaving geysers of wet or dry earth.

During World War I, aeroplanes ranged behind enemy lines to drop bombs on a haphazard basis and often achieved little more than moving some mud. Fighters took on the added role of strike aircraft during World War II, and made it routine. The RAF's Hawker Typhoon carried bombs and rockets on sorties against German targets on and behind the front lines. Near the end of the war, US Army Republic P-47 Thunderbolts flew on air-to-ground strikes. One pilot used the term 'Angels Zero', a reference to (almost) zero

---

340
FRANCE/UNITED KINGDOM 🇫🇷 🇬🇧
SEPECAT Jaguar

Designed by the consortium of British Aerospace and Dassault-Breguet, the **Jaguar** first flew in September 1968. A 'joint buy' for the *Armée de l'Air* and the RAF, it has performed extremely well since entering service in May 1972 and June 1973 respectively.

The French **Jaguar-A** type single-seat tactical support/attack aircraft flew for the first time in October 1969. It retains twin DEFA cannon armament, rather than Aden guns as in the British aircraft, and can carry up to 4536 kg (10,000 lb) of external stores on five wing and fuselage pylons. Total production for the French ran to 200 aircraft, while the RAF received 202.

To attract export orders, the **Jaguar International**, based on the **'S'**

tactical support version, made its maiden flight in October 1969. Since then it has been sold to a number of South American and Arab nations.

In line with France's policy of retaining an independent nuclear capability, a number of *Armée de l'Air* Jaguars are allocated a nuclear strike role using the AN-52 free-fall tactical bomb, probably without other stores except external fuel tanks to extend range and increase speed out of the target area.

Specification
SEPECAT Jaguar-A
Type: single-seat tactical strike bomber
Powerplant: two 3313-kg (7,305-lb)

Rolls-Royce/Turbomeca Adour turbofans
Performance: maximum speed 1320 km/h (820 mph); service ceiling 13750 m (45,000 ft); range 815 km (507 miles)
Dimensions: span 8.69 m (28 ft 6 in); length 15.52 m (50 ft 11 in); height

4.92 m (16 ft 1 in)
Weights: empty 8600 kg (15,000 lb); loaded 15500 kg (34,000 lb)
Armament: two 30-mm DEFA 553 cannon, plus up to 4536 kg (10,000 lb) of stores
Users: Ecuador, France, India, Nigeria, Oman and UK

altitude, for the title of his personal memoirs about strafing, bombing and rocketing the collapsing Third Reich.

Propeller-driven strike aircraft were still widely used during the Korean War (1950-3), when the Hawker Sea Fury and F-51 Mustang used bombs and rocket projectiles to cancel out the enemy's advantage in having a far larger army. The Republic F-84 Thunderjet was one of the first jet fighters assigned a strike role in combat, and some F-84s routinely carried 2,000-lb bombs and five-inch aerial rockets. Carrier-based strike aircraft in Korea included the prop-driven Douglas AD Skyraider and the jet Grumman F9F Panther.

Modern strike aircraft

The Vietnam War introduced the US Navy's Grumman A-6 Intruder, with radar and electronics to permit bombing at night and in poor weather. The Intruder remains the backbone of the US Navy's strike force. Newer types include the American Fairchild A-10A Thunderbolt II and the Soviet Sukhoi Su-25, or 'Frogfoot'.

In the 1990s, the Soviet Union has MiG and Sukhoi fighters assigned to strike duties. For the first time, some aircraft have been conceived for the strike mission, including the

A Mirage F1 fighter of the French air force launches an Armat anti-radar missile. Modern fighters are multi-purpose machines, equally ready to perform strike and ground attack missions as to get involved in a dogfight. Until the introduction of the Mirage 2000, the Mirage F1 was France's premier multi-role tactical fighter.

341

FRANCE

Dassault Mirage IV

In the very successful Mirage series of post-war military aircraft, the **Mirage IV** medium-range tactical bomber is by far the largest of the fighters and ground attack types. It was designed first and foremost to deliver atomic bombs with the French strategic air command.

First flying in June 1959, the Mirage IV had a delta configuration similar to that of the Mirage III, but was nearly 28 feet longer.

Dispersed on top security bases around the country, the **Mirage IVA** entered service in 1964. The force, three Escadres strong (some 45 aircraft out of a total of 62 built), was served by 12 KC-135 tankers. On an operational sortie, it was envisaged that two

Mirage IVs would accompany a tanker, one aircraft carrying the bomb and the other fuel, acting as a 'buddy' refueller after the tanker reached the limit of its penetration towards the target area.

To ensure that the bombers would be ready to go at short notice, 80 per cent operational readiness was maintained at all times, with one aircraft on 15-minute alert around the clock. To ensure a fast response if and when the scramble order came, the Mirage IV was provided with assisted take-off booster rockets. Currently, the remaining aircraft have been converted to a strategic reconnaissance role.

Specification
Dassault Mirage IV

Type: two-seat strategic bomber
Powerplant: two 7000-kg (15,423-lb) SNECMA Atar 9K turbojets
Performance: maximum speed 2340 km/h (1,454 mph); service ceiling 20000 m (65,620 ft); range 1240 km (770 miles)
Dimensions: span 11.85 m (38 ft 10 in); length 23.5 m (77 ft 1 in); height 5.4 m (17 ft 8 in)
Weights: empty 14500 kg (31,967 lb); loaded 33475 kg (73,800 lb)
Armament: one CEA AN-22 60-kiloton nuclear bomb, or up to 7257 kg (16,000 lb) on hardpoints
User: France

342

FRANCE

Dassault Mirage 2000N

A further variation on the well-proven Dassault delta theme, the **Mirage 2000** is the latest in a highly successful line of French interceptors and ground attack aircraft. The 2000 incorporates a fly-by-wire control system, which gives it unrivalled manoeuvrability, and is stressed to withstand high *g* forces in air combat.

Such agility makes the aircraft ideal for ground attack work; the ability to fly low and fast, deliver bombs on target and, if necessary, fight enemy interceptors on the way back to base makes for an economical and versatile weapon. Therefore, it is not surprising that the Mirage 2000 comes in at least five versions, including the two-seat **B** model trainer

For attack sorties, there is the **2000N**, which is primarily tasked with low-level strike with a wide range of conventional munitions, such as 'iron' bombs, runway denial and anti-personnel (cluster) bombs, as well as tactical nuclear weapons. In this last role, the 2000N would almost certainly carry one of two known French air-launched nuclear bombs, the 600-kg (1,322.75-lb) CEA AN-52. A free-fall bomb of conventional shape with cruciform tailfins, the AN-52 has a nuclear yield of between 14 and 18 kilotons. It would almost certainly be attached to the fuselage centreline pylon for a nuclear strike mission. The 2000N is also configured to carry the ASMP stand-off missile.

Specification
Dassault Mirage 2000N
Type: nuclear/conventional strike
Powerplant: one 9000-kg (19,840-lb) SNECMA M53 afterburning turbojet
Performance: maximum speed 2440 km/h (1,918 mph); service ceiling 18300 m (60,000 ft); range 1850 km (1,150 miles)
Dimensions: span 9 m (29 ft 6 in); length 15.3 m (50 ft 3 in); height 5.15 m (16 ft 10 in)
Weights: empty 7636 kg (16,835 lb); loaded 11761 kg (25,928 lb)
Armament: 5000 kg (11,025 lb) stores
User: France

First revealed in the late 1970s, the Sukhoi Su-24 'Fencer' is a highly capable aircraft designed for the same mission as the General Dynamics F-111 and the Panavia Tornado.

very impressive Sukhoi Su-24 (called 'Fencer' by NATO) which first flew in 1970 and equips a dozen regiments (400 aircraft) at Russian bases. The Su-24 is about 50 per cent bigger than fighters like the MiG-23 and MiG-29, and even with the end of the Cold War is poised for all-weather strike missions against NATO military installations and air bases. The 'Fencer' is not as large as the American F-111 or as up-to-date as the British Tornado.

The General Dynamics F-111, unofficially called the 'Aardvark', first flew in prototype form on 21 December 1964, has served since the late 1960s, and equips four American fighter wings. With both an internal bomb bay and provision for ordnance beneath its wings, the F-111 is best known for its long-range

343 McDonnell Douglas F-15E Eagle

USA

A logical development of the single-seat air superiority Eagle, the **F-15E** ground attack version has two seats – similar to the Eagle trainer. There the similarity all but ends, for the Echo model is a dedicated 'mud mover' with a secondary air combat capability. It first flew as an updated B model demonstrator with the rear cockpit incorporating four CRT displays for radar, weapons selection and monitoring of enemy systems.

Production aircraft for the US Air Force have further modifications, including a wide-field-of-vision HUD and three CRT displays, a flight control system with automatic terrain-following, and laser-enhanced inertial navigation. High-resolution radar

permits high-speed target attack at night and in adverse weather conditions, a task enhanced by LANTIRN and wide-field FLIR pods. A revised engine bay layout allows the installation of either General Electric F110 or Pratt & Whitney F100 engines.

Conformal pallets restore some of the internal fuel space lost when the new avionics suite was installed, and these are fitted with hardpoints for missiles. This extends the **F-15E's** capability to the air-to-air combat role, although the primary mission is attack, using guided and unguided low-drag bombs.

The US Air Force has a requirement for 200 F-15Es; the first wing became operational in late 1989.

Specification
McDonnell Douglas F-15E Eagle
Type: two-seat attack fighter
Powerplant: two 10855-kg (23,500-lb) thrust GE F110/P&W F100 turbofans
Performance: max speed at sea level over 800 knots (1482 km/h; 921 mph); combat radius 1270 km (790 miles)
Dimensions: span 13.05 m (42 ft 8 in); length 19.43 m (63 ft 9 in); height 5.63 m (18 ft 4 in)
Weights: empty 13700 kg (30,300 lb); loaded 25050 kg (55,270 lb)
Armament: one 20-mm cannon and up to 12265 kg (24,500 lb) of stores
User: USA

344 Sukhoi Su-22 'Fitter'

FORMER USSR

Believing variable geometry to be highly adaptable to ground attack aircraft, Sukhoi developed and flew a test version of the Su-7 in 1966. Impressed Soviet air force officials ordered production of a new battlefield support aircraft almost immediately.

The **Su-17** entered Soviet service in 1971, to be followed by the **Su-20** which, like all 'Fitter' variants, features only partial variable geometry, with only the outer wing panels being movable in flight. The similar **Su-22 'Fitter-F'** was offered for export in 1977. The Su-22 had markedly revised fuselage contours, with a faired-in cockpit canopy and distinctive dorsal 'hump', a dorsal intake (on the **Su-22 M-4**), a ventral strake under the rear fuselage,

and four rather than two wing fences, as on the Su-17. Peru was the initial customer for an aircraft with minor changes compared with the Soviet model. The other Su-22 variants are identified as: **'Fitter-G'**, an export counterpart of the 'Fitter-F' but with R-29B engines; **'Fitter-J'**, generally similar to **'Fitter-H'** but with a Tumansky engine, a more angular dorsal fin and Atoll AAM capability; and **'Fitter-K'**, the Soviet air force Su-22 M-4 and equivalent export models. As one of the most adaptable contemporary Soviet designs, over 1,000 examples remain in service.

Specification
Sukhoi Su-22 'Fitter-F'

Type: ground attack aircraft
Powerplant: one 11340-kg (25,000-lb) Lyulka AL-21F-3 afterburning turbojet
Performance: max speed 2305 km/h (1,432 mph); service ceiling 18000 m (59,050 ft); range 630 km (391 miles)
Dimensions: span 14 m (45 ft 11 in); length 18.75 m (61 ft 6 in); height

4.75 m (15 ft 7 in)
Weights: empty 10000 kg (22,046 lb); loaded 14000 kg (30,865 lb)
Armament: two 30-mm NR-30 cannon and up to 5000 kg (11,023 lb) of external stores
Users: Germany, Hungary, Libya, Peru, Poland, USSR and Yemen

The General Dynamics F-111 combined high performance and advanced electronics to an unprecedented degree when it entered service in the 1960s. After initial teething troubles, it proved to be one of the most effective strike aircraft in the world – a position it held for a decade until the Sukhoi Su-24 and the Panavia Tornado made their appearances.

Combat Comparison

Two of the most important strike aircraft currently in service are the General Dynamics F-111 and the Sukhoi Su-24 'Fencer'. Both have side-by-side cockpit seating and variable-geometry wings, both are crammed with electronics, and both can carry a considerable weapons load.

strikes against terrorist-related targets in Libya in April 1986.

The strike aircraft of the 1990s, as far as the RAF is concerned, is the Panavia Tornado, also used by Germany, Saudi Arabia and Italy. First flown on 10 July 1979, the Tornado was designed from the outset for the strike role. On a medium-range strike mission, the two-seat Tornado can carry eight 1,000-lb bombs under its fuselage, protect itself from enemy detection with advanced ECM (electronic countermeasures) gear, and fly 480 miles to hit an enemy airfield, bridge, or supply convoy.

The Tornado, 'Fencer' and F-111 all have variable-geometry wings that can be swept back for flight at very high speeds in combat or kept forward for low-speed landing and take-off. All have costly packages of electronic wizardry, enabling them to fly at treetop level at very high speed ('terrain following'), and to locate targets and aim weapons.

Aircraft designed for the strike mission receive less attention – and less funding – than those intended for air-to-air combat, so future warplanes may be like the American McDonnell F/A-18 Hornet, which has a 'dual role'

capability – able to fly strike missions *and* fight in air-to-air combat. Among land-based warplanes, the familiar F-111 has been joined by limited numbers of the F-15E Eagle (originally called 'Strike Eagle'), the latest warplane to fill the 'dual role' bill.

Britain and the European allies can be expected to stick with updated versions of the Tornado. An improvement programme is likely, as well, for the Soviet Su-24 'Fencer'.

Scheduled to fly in 1991, the American General Dynamics A-12 Avenger II was to be the US Navy's standard medium attack aircraft to replace the A-6 Intruder in the strike mission. Little was said about what the A-12 looked like, how it would employ 'stealth' to confound enemy radar and missiles, and what its capabilities were. Just as the Tornado is the strike aircraft to arouse envy among pilots everywhere today, the A-12 was intended to be *the* strike aircraft of the 21st Century, using ever more advanced technical marvels.

The heart of the F-111's attack systems is its terrain-following radar, which enables the fighter to fly low-level missions in zero visibility and still hit targets accurately.

The Sukhoi Su-24 was developed for long-range, all-weather attack. It was designed with unrefuelled range that enables the aircraft to mount strikes from Soviet bases against targets as far afield as the north of Scotland, the South of Italy, and anywhere in the Middle East. Marginally smaller than the F-111, the 'Fencer' nevertheless packs a considerable punch.

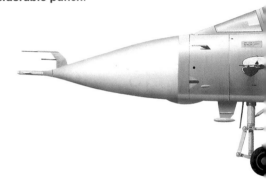

346   USA

General Dynamics F-111

One of the most successful strike aircraft in the US Air Force inventory, the variable-geometry **F-111** appeared to be a disaster when it was designed as a multi-role aircraft able to fly any mission. When the US Navy (and the RAF) declined to place orders, the USAF had little choice but to persevere with development. The **F-111A** eventually entered Air Force service in 1967 and although it was highly sophisticated and drew heavily for flight data on read-outs from computerised systems, the idea still didn't seem to work when a limited deployment to South East Asia took place in 1969.

First flown in December 1964, the General Dynamics F-111 had several never-before-seen features: variable-sweep 'swing' wings, augmented turbofan engines, and terrain-following radar. The version sold to Australia was the F-111C, which had a higher operating weight than US Air Force models, thanks to stronger landing gear and longer wings.

345 FORMER USSR

Sukhoi Su-24 'Fencer'

The **Su-24** was directly influenced by the US TFX programme that led to the F-111; the Soviet air force wanted similar capability and believed that this would come from a swing-wing design. The prototype flew in 1969 and production aircraft entered service in 1974.

Soviet estimates proved true enough – the Su-24 emerged as one of the most capable of combat aircraft, with a useful range, variable weapons load, and advanced electronic countermeasures and early warning systems. It was smaller and lighter than the F-111, and has been built in at least five versions to date. These include: **'Fencer-A'**, which has a rectangular rear fuselage box housing for the jet nozzles; **'Fencer-B'**, with further revised rear fuselage contours and a larger braking parachute than standard; **'Fencer-C'**, a sub-type introduced in 1981 with detailed external changes, including multiple nose probes instead of the previous one; **'Fencer-D'**,

introduced in 1983 with improved inflight-refuelling capability using a single, lengthened probe, a slightly longer nose, 'kinked' fin leading edge, large overwing fences and extended wing root glove pylons, probably for the carriage of the large Kedge air-to-surface missiles; and **'Fencer-E'**, a reconnaissance version of 'Fencer-D'.

'Fencer' remains an important element in Soviet air defence and there are currently some 800 in service.

Specification
Sukhoi Su-24 'Fencer'
Type: two-seat attack bomber
Powerplant: two 18960-kg (27,500-lb) Lyulka AL-21F-3 afterburning turbojets
Performance: maximum speed at sea level 1470 km/h (913 mph); service ceiling 17500 m (57,400 ft); range 1800 km (1,115 miles)

Supersonic at sea level, the Su-24 can fly at twice the speed of sound at altitude. But since carrying weapons increases drag considerably, missions will probably be flown at high subsonic speeds. Inflight refuelling extends range indefinitely, however.

Dimensions: span spread 17.25 m (56 ft 7 in); swept 10 m (32 ft 9 in); length 20.5 m (67 ft 3 in); height 4.97 m (16 ft 3.75 in)
Weights: empty 11800 kg (39,700 lb); loaded 29000 kg (64,000 lb)
Armament: one 30-mm Gatling cannon, plus up to 8000 kg (17,635 lb) of external stores
Users: Libya, Syria and USSR

Unlike the F-111, the 'Fencer' can carry weapons under its fuselage. Eight hardpoints are available for bombs, nuclear weapons, unguided rockets, fuel tanks, or short- and medium-range air-to-surface missiles like the AS-7 'Kerry', AS-10 'Karen', AS-11 'Kilter', AS-12 'Kegler' and AS-14 'Kedge'.

Like the F-111, the Sukhoi Su-24 has a two-seat cockpit, with side-by-side seating for pilot and weapons operator/navigator. It has a specially developed long-range navigational system and an electro-optical weapons delivery system, accurate to within 15 metres even in zero visibility.

The USAF and General Dynamics initiated fixes, and gradually the aircraft came right and began flying the kind of mission few others were capable of, particularly at night. With everything looking better, the F-111 went to Vietnam a second time. Tasked with night strikes on prime targets in Hanoi and Haiphong, crews used terrain-following radar to guide the F-111 unerringly over mountains to bore right into the target.

It was widely said that an F-111 with all the taps out could not be detected by North Vietnam's gunnery radars and that it even gave SAMs a good run for their money. The aircraft also performed well in the Eldorado Canyon raid on Libya, and today there are some 320

left in service. Current updating programmes, which include bringing **FB-111**s up to **F-111G** standard, are not expected to be completed until 1994, giving the type a lifespan into the 21st century.

Specification
General Dynamics F-111
Type: two-seat tactical strike bomber
Powerplant: two 11385-kg (25,100-lb) Pratt & Whitney TF30-100 afterburning turbofans
Performance: maximum speed 2335 km/h (1,450 mph) at 11000 m (36,000 ft); service ceiling 18290 m (60,000 ft); range 4707 km (2,925 miles)

The F-111's robust landing gear allows it to use rough fields, but the layout of the gear and the small internal bomb bay mean that there is no room for underfuselage hardpoints. Even so, the six wing pylons can carry up to 14 tons of stores.

Dimensions: span spread 19.2 m (63 ft); swept 9.74 m (31 ft 11 in); length 22.4 m (73 ft 6 in); height 5.22 m (17 ft 1 in)
Weights: empty 21537 kg (47,481 lb); loaded 45360 kg (100,000 lb)
Armament: one B43 nuclear weapon and one M61 gun internally, plus up to 14288 kg (31,500 lb) of external stores
User: USA

The F-111C supplied to the Royal Australian Air Force had low-thrust engines with the longer wing designed for the FB-111 nuclear bomber. Four of the Australian aircraft were modified to carry a multi-sensor reconnaissance pack in place of weapons.

The F-111 introduced side-by-side seating for modern strike aircraft. In place of the normal ejection seats, the whole cockpit of the F-111 is designed as an escape capsule with its own parachutes. The escape capsule can serve as a boat or a survival shelter.

THE PENETRATORS

Modern radar and missile defences are very effective, and the only way to get through them is to minimise the enemy's chances of detecting an intruder. Until recently, that has meant flying very fast, very low. But with the advent of stealth, all that may change.

A pair of Jaguar strike aircraft blast over the desert sands of Oman. High-speed, low-level performance is the key to successful strike operations in these days of sophisticated air defences, and the Jaguar is in its element flying at close to the speed of sound only a few metres above the ground.

An extremely important element in modern battle is the deep strike behind enemy lines, designed to cut communications and to hamper the movement of reinforcements. Unfortunately, modern missile and electronic defence systems are designed to block such missions by large manned aircraft, so they must be flown in such a way as to elude those defences.

It is not a new problem, however. During World War II, both the Luftwaffe and the Royal Air Force flew intruder missions, using high-performance light bombers like the Mosquito and the Junkers Ju-88 to strike at bomber bases. Heavily-armed American aircraft like the Douglas A-20 Havoc and the Northrop P-61 Black Widow were in a similar mould.

After the war, the intruder mission was flown by tactical bombers like the Canberra or converted fighters like the Republic F-84 Thunderchief, striking deep behind enemy lines in missions which fit in somewhere between the tactical missions over the battlefield and the strategic tasks involving flying deep into the enemy's homeland.

In the early 1950s, it was realised that high-speed, low-level flight was the only way to penetrate in creasingly effective air defences. For a time, flying at twice the speed of sound was *de rigeur*. However, supersonic speed is almost impossible at low level, especially when a fighter is bombed-up. Indeed, when the Blackburn Buccaneer first appeared it was scorned for its subsonic performance; nevertheless, it can fly long distances with a two-ton bomb load, at higher speeds than most of its supersonic rivals, and with half the fuel consumption.

In the strike mission, good low-level speed and a reasonable weapons load are more important than high-altitude performance. Yet, to survive, a strike fighter needs much more. If you are not detected by the enemy, he will not shoot you down. You can load your aircraft with electronic systems designed to detect hostile radars or oncoming missiles, and add fast-reacting countermeasures to jam or decoy such systems. But the way ahead is in the application of stealth technology. A strike fighter made of radar-absorbent materials, and designed to reflect the minimum of electromagnetic or infra-red energy, will have the best chance of getting through and destroying the target.

Above: A Republic P-47 Thunderbolt attacks a German ammunition truck. At such low level, the fighter is in real danger of being hit by debris when the vehicle explodes.

World War II intruders

Air power came of age during World War II. Most of the missions which now comprise air combat were developed between 1939 and 1945. Air power was used for national defence, counter-air missions, strategic bombing, close air support, reconnaissance, and many other tasks. In the last two years of the war, Allied fighter-bombers were roaming the skies of France and Germany, almost at will. Their targets were trains, road convoys, airfields, troop concentrations, and all the many and varied activities that take place behind an enemy's front lines. Among the most interesting missions were those of the intruder — with heavily-armed light bombers insinuating themselves into enemy formations, and attacking enemy airfields as the unsuspecting aircraft came in to land. A number of special operations were flown, involving high-speed, low-level penetration of enemy territory to make 'surgical' strikes at specific targets. The Mosquito missions against the Gestapo headquarters at Amiens, the Hague and Copenhagen were of this type, as were the strikes flown by American bombers against Japanese ports in the South Pacific.

Above: A Douglas A-20 attack bomber is hit by anti-aircraft fire during a 1944 raid on a Japanese naval base on the north coast of New Guinea.

Right: High explosive rockets are loaded onto a de Havilland Mosquito fighter. This fast, twin-engined machine was extensively used on intruder missions.

Post-war nuclear strike

Air combat changed dramatically in the years following World War II, thanks to the turbojet engine and the rapid development of nuclear weapons. Britain's Canberra was one of the first jet-powered light bombers, and was equipped to perform the penetration mission like a jet-age Mosquito. The North American B-45 Tornado and the Republic F-84 Thunderstreak were designed for the tactical nuclear mission. In the event of war, they were meant to unleash the power of the atom in enemy rear areas, command centres, and on lines of communication. Soviet strike aircraft of the period included the Canberra-equivalent Ilyushin Il-28 'Beagle' light bomber and the Yakovlev Yak-25 'Brewer' multi-purpose fighter. But advanced though they were for their time, they were quickly outmoded, though not replaced. The pace of aircraft development in the 1950s was unrelenting; by the end of the decade, Mach-2 strike fighters like the massive Republic F-105 Thunderchief were operational.

Left: The English Electric Canberra was one of the world's first operational jet bombers, and proved to be an all-time classic aircraft design. Highly manoeuvrable at low level, it was built in many variants, including intruder versions with fighter-style cockpits. These were intended to perform long-range night interdiction missions.

Above: The Republic F-84F Thunderstreak was one of the first single-seat fighters designed to carry nuclear weapons. This example is armed with a Bullpup command-guided missile.

Above: Ilyushin Il-28 'Beagle' light bombers pass over a 'Frosch' class assault ship of the East German navy during Baltic exercises. The 'Beagle' could carry three tons of bombs or a pair of torpedoes internally. In service since the late 1940s, the Il-28 provided the main striking power for Warsaw Pact air forces well into the 1960s, and large numbers of the type remain in service as bombers with the Chinese air force and navy.

Left: The Yak-28 'Brewer' was developed in parallel with the 'Firebar' all-weather fighter, and first appeared in the early 1960s. Equipped with a prominent bombing radar under the fuselage, and an internal weapons bay, the 'Brewer' was almost certainly designed for tactical nuclear strike. The glazed navigator's station in the nose was typical of Soviet aircraft of the period.

The electronics revolution

Low-level performance became the key to successful penetration of enemy defences in the 1960s. The British spent millions on the development of the TSR Mk 2 bomber, which was to carry a large bomb load at treetop height supersonically. Equipped with advanced navigation systems and terrain-following radar, it was a highly advanced package, but was cancelled by a Labour government less than five months after its first flight. The American F-111 swing-wing bomber was of equally revolutionary design; although it suffered teething troubles when it eventually entered service, it was for almost 20 years the most advanced strike aircraft in the world. France's Mirage IV was a large supersonic bomber which first flew in the 1960s. Intended for the nuclear strike role, the Mirage can also carry conventional weapons. The supersonic Tupolev Tu-22 'Blinder', developed by the Soviets in the 1950s, was first seen in 1961. Possibly designed as a strategic weapon system, it lacked true strategic range, and so was most likely to be assigned to deep strike operations.

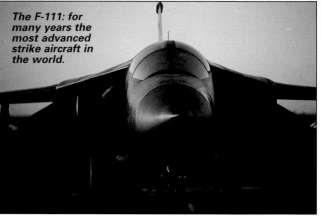

The F-111: for many years the most advanced strike aircraft in the world.

Left: The 'facetted' fuselage of the F-117A 'Stealth' fighter reflects no more radar energy than a bird, making it possible for the aircraft to slip undetected through enemy radar networks.

Stealth

As air defences become more and more effective, the future of strike aircraft lies with stealth technology. By careful design and by using advanced radar-absorbent materials, you can reduce an aircraft's radar cross-section to that of a small bird. The American B-1B bomber reflects one per cent of the energy mirrored by the old B-52, and the latest designs like the F-117A 'Stealth' fighter and the B-2 bomber have less than five per cent of the B-1's cross-section. With low infra-red (heat) signatures, quiet engines, and a minimum of give-away avionics, such designs are intended to be virtually undetectable, especially at night.

The Russian Federation and Europeans appear to have a different attitude. Rather than spend fortunes to produce dedicated stealth aircraft, they prefer to use stealth technology where appropriate on more conventional designs. Although such machines might have larger radar signatures than the F-117 or the B-2, they can be acquired for $50 million apiece, rather than the $1 billion that each B-2 bomber costs.

'AARDVARKS' OVER HANOI

Above: Two of the first F-111s deployed under Operation Combat Lancer are seen en route to Vietnam. The F-111 was to undergo a troubled baptism of fire.

Below: An F-111 acts as bombing guide to a pair of US Air Force Phantoms. The F-111 was equipped with the advanced navigation and bombing aids the F-4s lacked.

Known as the 'Aardvark' from its long, drooping nose, the F-111 had swing wings, and the most advanced electronics ever fitted to a warplane. It should have been an immediate success, but the F-111's first combat missions were disastrous.

On 28 March 1968, in the first combat mission by a General Dynamics F-111A, an aircraft laden with two ALQ-87 jamming pods and 24 Mk 82 bombs lifted off from Takhli, Thailand, to assault a target in North Vietnam. This F-111A (66-0022) vanished for ever. On 22 April 1968, another attempt was made to hurl the F-111A into battle. Now, another F-111A (68-0024) headed north, and also disappeared.

It was a grim and frightening start for Operation Combat Lancer, the US Air Force's controversial baptism of fire for the F-111. Under Colonel Ivan H. Dethman, a cigar-smoking, tyre-kicking combat veteran, the 428th Tactical Fighter Squadron on 17 March 1968 had ferried six F-111As from Nellis AFB, Nevada,

to Takhli, where the strike aircraft were detached to the 355th Tactical Fighter Wing, then flying Republic F-105D Thunderchiefs in the campaign against North Vietnam, known as 'Rolling Thunder'. As the men settled in amid the heat and red dust at Takhli, it was now more than a decade since the first studies aimed at developing the costly and trouble-prone F-111, seven years since Secretary of Defense Robert S. MacNamara had ballyhooed production of what was then perceived as the bi-service TFX multi-role strike aircraft, and four years since the maiden flight of the aeroplane on 21 December 1964. The F-111, so unloved that it was never assigned a popular name, dubbed 'Aardvark' by enthusiasts but not

Above: Inflight refuelling has changed war in the air more than any other technique developed since the end of World War II. Topping-up in the air meant that F-111s could fly for long distances at gas-guzzling low level without the need to conserve fuel.

Above, right: Four F-111s in diamond formation make a flypast at Takhli Royal Thai Air Force Base as they arrive on the first Combat Lancer deployment in 1968. Three out of six aircraft would fail to return from missions over North Vietnam.

Right: Seen over the Nevada desert before deployment to South East Asia, the F-111 was, by a long way, the most advanced strike aircraft in the world, and a lot of hopes were riding on its success in Vietnam.

by crews, had failed totally and abysmally in the crucible of combat. Dethman's men, his ACs (aircraft commanders) and YOTs ('You over there!', the term for an F-111A weapon system officer) were demoralised by the unexplained loss of half their strike force; for by late April 1968, a third F-111A had travelled one-way into North Vietnam. Instead of proving that the aircraft design had merit, the theatre deployment had, instead, yielded gloom and doom.

Failure a mystery

It should not have been that way. Indeed, the F-111A seemed ideally constructed to deal punishing blows to the North

Vietnamese. With its 6743-km (4,190-mile) range, it was the only strike aircraft able to carry a full load of ordnance 'downtown' (to Hanoi) without inflight refuelling. Its advanced Litton LND-21/A navigation and weapons delivery system permitted deep penetration by lone aircraft – without escort, and with no back-up from tankers, ECM, airborne early warning, or any other support planes – giving a 'lone wolf' capability matched in all the world only by the Grumman A-6A Intruder. The F-111A could carry up to 14424 kg (31,800 lb) of 'iron' bombs (usually the proximity-fused 227-kg/500-lb Mk 82 Snakeye) on a night or bad-weather, terrain-hugging mission

deep into Ho Chi Minh's homeland. It was clearly an effective warplane, even if ACs and YOTs grumbled unceasingly about its unorthodox, side-by-side seating.

The number four symbolises bad luck in Asian societies. On attempt number four, a Combat Lancer crew strapped in, hurtled aloft from Takhli before dawn on 28 April 1968, and under radio silence bored north-east towards a target in North Vietnam, thought to be the Hai Duong rail complex. As on the initial mission, 24 Snakeyes hung from multiple ejector racks on the F-111A's pylons, while twin ALQ-87 jammer pods were ready to disrupt enemy radar

transmissions. Again, two men in the unique forward-fuselage escape pod of the 'Aardvark' (which obviated the need for parachutes or ejection seats) were heading out on an ultra-low-level, ground-skimming mission of the kind which had already claimed three aircraft and six buddies.

Fourth time lucky

This time, everything went like clockwork. The sophisticated navigation system of the F-111A permitted ground-hugging tactics which rendered the strike aircraft invisible to North Vietnam's field-sweep radar. Since the F-111A's endurance was so much greater than that of the F-105D or McDonnell F-4C, fuel

consumption (although ravenous 'on the deck') was not a problem. The AC and YOT, relatively comfortable in their spacious cockpit, flew towards their target with the radar homing and warning system utterly silent – evidence that they were undetected. No AA fire, no SAMs, no MiGs, rose to challenge them. The two men were lugging a substantial payload at high subsonic cruise at treetop level against the heaviest defences the world had ever seen, and nobody seemed to know they were coming!

Fatal flaw discovered

Some 51 more, equally successful, missions were flown by Colonel Dethman's Combat Lancer F-111As. After the end of the war – too late to help with the planning in 1968 – it was established that abrupt tailplane failure caused by fatigue at a welding fault, not enemy action, could throw the F-111A into an uncontrollable fatal manoeuvre. Dethman's force was withdrawn with the temporary bombing halt on 31 October 1968, and in 1969 all 'Aardvarks' were grounded to correct this flaw. But F-111s returned with a vengeance for the 1972 campaign against North Vietnam, called 'Linebacker'.

Captain Peter A. Messenies, F-111A pilot, recalls a mission to the outskirts of Hanoi: "We were at an altitude of 250 feet, moving at Mach .87 in a region of odd-shaped ridges and peaks, and we were in clouds and haze for the final 14 minutes of our run-in to the target. . ."

Although four F-111s were lost in combat in 1972 (67-0063, 67-0068, 67-0092, 67-0094) and one more in Laotian operations after the end of the war (67-0111), the unpopular 'Aardvark' had proved itself as a long-range strike aircraft with unmatched night/all-weather capability. F-111s assaulted fuel dumps, railyards and bridges. Some, under the 'Igloo White' programme, seeded enemy terrain with para-dropped acoustic sensors that detected North Vietnamese troop movements. F-111As from the 428th and 430th Tactical Fighter Squadrons supported the massive 'Christmas bombing' by Boeing B-52s in the Hanoi/Haiphong region in December 1972. These two squadrons flew 4,030 sorties in five months, mostly at low level in bad weather, and 2.5 million kg (5.5 million lb) of bombs were carried to enemy targets. In the end, despite its poor beginning, the F-111 dealt out crippling punishment, helped force North Vietnam to a settlement, and (when overall mission sorties are counted) suffered fewer losses per combat hour than any other aircraft type in South East Asia.

Above: Swooping low over the North Vietnamese terrain, the F-111 was to give the US Air Force the ability to strike where and when it liked, whatever the time of day or weather.

Right: The F-111 is also a nuclear bomber, and in its FB-111 form it serves with SAC (Strategic Air Command). In the nuclear strike role it is essential that the F-111 be supported by tankers.

Below: An F-111 comes in to land at Takhli in 1972. After its disastrous combat debut, the F-111 was to mature into a reliable and effective weapons system.

The space shuttle Columbia *lifts off* on a satellite launch mission. The use of space *has revolutionised reconnaissance.*

Left: Shuttle specialists prepare a satellite for launch. Spy satellites are now the best strategic reconnaissance system for the superpowers, being nearly invulnerable to attack from the ground.

High-Flying Photographers

The camera and the aeroplane both became practical propositions at the beginning of this century, and during World War I they were used in combination to shoot millions of pictures of the Western Front. During World War II, aerial photo-reconnaissance added immeasurably to the information available to ground commanders and planners. Since 1945, it has remained an important military tool, in spite of the growth of other reconnaissance platforms and sensors. Photo-reconnaissance has also expanded its scope, being used for national strategic tasks. At the height of the Cold War, NATO's reconnaissance planes made daring and dangerous overflights of Eastern Europe and the Soviet Union, while in recent years they have been used to verify arms agreements and to monitor trouble spots around the world.

1955
Lockheed U-2/TR-1

The TR-1 is the latest development of the U-2. Designed as a tactical reconnaissance aircraft, its task is to stay in friendly airspace while looking obliquely deep into hostile territory.

1964
Lockheed SR-71A

The SR-71 was one of the most dramatic aircraft ever to take to the skies. The fastest and highest flying jet aircraft ever built, it was virtually immune to interception.

fighters and bombers are replacing aircraft such as the RF-4C in the tactical reconnaissance role. Remotely-piloted drones will be increasingly used, and satellites will continue to make a vital contribution to the strategic collection of intelligence. But an aeroplane with a pilot can go places and do things that a drone or satellite cannot – so some kind of spy aircraft will continue to be not just important but necessary.

Another product of Lockheed's renowned 'Skunk Works' is the F-117A Night-hawk 'stealth' fighter, tested under tight security on the USAF's vast Nellis ranges. And like the F-117A, other secret aircraft are rumoured to be under test in the Nevada desert, including a mystery ship, never acknowledged by the US government, called the Aurora. Future spy aircraft pilots will have ever more futuristic ships to fly.

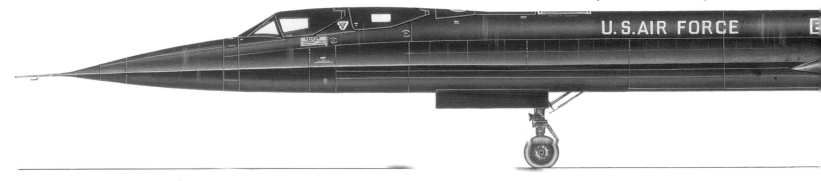

U.S.AIR FORCE

 **1916**

Royal Aircraft Factory RE.8

The RE.8 was known as the 'Harry Tate' after a famous musical hall performer of the time. It was the RFC's main reconnaissance aircraft in 1917 and 1918, with more than 4,000 being built. It was slower than the German scouts, and had to be escorted by Allied fighters on its photographic missions over the front line.

 **1942**

Spitfire PR.Mk XI

The Spitfire PR.Mk XI was developed from the Mk IX fighter. Unarmed, and with a streamlined windscreen, it was capable of 417 mph at 24,500 feet, and could climb to 40,000 feet.

1943

Arado Ar 234 'Blitz'

The Arado 234 was the world's first operational jet bomber, but its first missions in 1944 saw the pioneering jet making reconnaissance flights over England. Capable of 460 mph at altitude, it was almost impossible to intercept.

Below: Lockheed's amazing U-2 was a product of Clarence 'Kelly' Johnson's 'Skunk Works' design team. Proposed in 1954, and first flying in 1955, it was used at the height of the Cold War to spy on the Soviet Union. Operating at heights of 70,000 feet, it was thought to be invulnerable, until Francis 'Gary' Powers was shot down in 1960.

For more than a quarter of a century, the SR-71 made its Mach 3 reconnaissance flights over the hotspots of the world and around the periphery of the USSR. Even on retirement, in 1990, it remained the ultimate in high-speed, high-altitude performance.

Keith Fretwell.

EYE IN THE SKY

Above: A false-colour satellite image of the Chesapeake Bay shows the cities of Washington and Baltimore in blue, with cultivated land in red. Such images can be used by analysts to gather strategic information, such as the kinds of harvests expected or the amount of industry in an area.

Left: Amazing though satellites are, it must be remembered that they are looking at objects more than 100 miles away. There are some things which need closer observation; these call for a spyplane. The Lockheed TR-1 can be fitted with a variety of sensors including cameras, infra-red, radar and communications intercept gear.

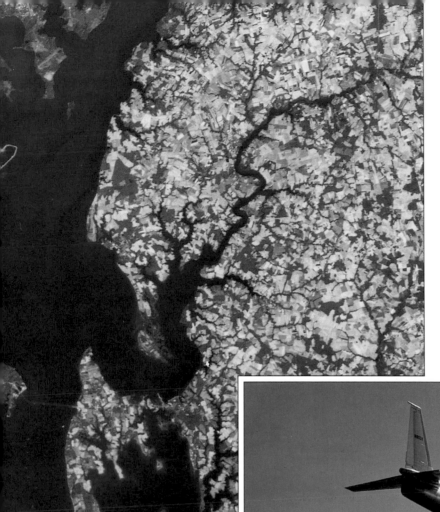

Strategic reconnaissance

The primary purpose of a strategic reconnaissance system is to enable national command authorities to assess the military capacity of a target nation during peacetime, and to continue such a task if war breaks out. This kind of operation, carried out continuously over long periods of time, is more properly known as surveillance. Strategic reconnaissance platforms need to gather as much information about as wide an area as possible in a single pass, so they have in the past tended to be high-altitude craft such as the Lockheed U-2 and the amazing Lockheed SR-71.

Nowadays the bulk of the intelligence used in strategic planning comes from satellites. These look for a wide range of signs of military expansion, from major troop movements or the setting-up of new missile batteries to militarily significant economic changes, such as factories producing ammunition going on to a three-shift, 24-hour production schedule.

Knowing the enemy enables you to deal with him, and spies in the sky are the best means of getting that knowledge.

Wellington once said that the art of being a successful general was "guessing correctly what lay on the other side of the hill". The Iron Duke's job would have been made much easier if he had had aerial reconnaissance. Since man first took to the skies in balloons, he has used his new vantage point to gain information in war. But the days of the man in the balloon drawing maps and writing notes have long gone.

The first increase in capability came during World War I, when cameras were taken aloft. Since then, photography has become just one of a whole battery of sensors used to take the guesswork out of intelligence.

Modern reconnaissance has split into two main areas of activity. Strategic reconnaissance is designed to help create the 'big picture' for high commands and national authorities, while tactical reconnaissance is dedicated to providing operational and tactical information for ground forces.

Intelligence comes in three varieties. **Humint** (human intelligence) is the stuff of spy novels, with agents in target countries gathering a wide variety of information, but which has little to do with spy aircraft. **Imagery** involves obtaining photographic, infra-red, or radar images of particular areas. Aircraft and satellites are the major means of obtaining such information. Lastly, the vast field of **Sigint** (signals intelligence) covers communications intelligence, electronic intelligence and telemetry intelligence, among others.

In peace or war, good intelligence is vital. Without it you are like a man searching for a black cat in a darkened room: you know it is there, somewhere, but finding it will be down to blind chance. Reconnaissance is the light that will illuminate your efforts.

It is probable that the most advanced spy satellites bear some relation to designs for space telescopes. They are so powerful that they can read car number plates from their orbits hundreds of miles into space.

Tactical reconnai⟨s⟩

The boundary between strategic and tactica⟨l⟩ reconnaissance is a little blurred. In genera⟨l⟩ reconnaissance is carried out on behalf of th⟨e⟩ commander, and is usually provided by varia⟨nt⟩ high-performance aircraft. But strategic syst⟨ems⟩ be used for tactical purposes: SR-71s made M⟨ach⟩ altitude reconnaissance flights to check out h⟨ostile⟩ defences before US military actions in the 198⟨0s⟩ like Grenada, Libya and Panama. Tactical recon⟨naissance⟩ rarely involves surveillance, with aircraft instea⟨d⟩ tasked with providing intelligence about a specif⟨ic⟩ over a short period of time.

Left: The Lockheed U-2 was the first 'invulnerable' spyplane, but it spurred Soviet SAM development until they managed to shoot one down in 1960.

Below: A Titan 37 rocket rises spectacularly from the US Air Force's Space Launch Complex 40. The Titan was originally an ICBM design, but is now used to lift heavy satellite loads into orbit.

⟨...⟩el
⟨...⟩ be used as
⟨...⟩pidly than
⟨...⟩ wings.
⟨...⟩ver 45000
⟨...⟩ut fuel
⟨...⟩t 130
⟨...⟩00°F).

AIR FORCE
COMPLEX 40

Above: An RAF Jaguar GR.Mk 1 switches on its afterburners as it dives down to make a low-level recce pass. The reconnaissance sensors are carried in the pod under the fuselage.

Right: Black-and-white film remains the most effective imaging medium for reconnaissance. Interpreters are able to analyse images like this to give details of enemy units and weapons.

Imagery

The basic and oldest-established form of reconnaissance involves making images of a target area. In the old ballooning days it involved a man with a pencil and paper making sketches of enemy fortifications, but soon aircraft were carrying cameras into the skies. Today, the camera shooting black-and-white film is still the most important reconnaissance tool, although it is a far cry from the ones you would use to take your holiday snaps. Long focal lengths, high-technology optics and superfine film mean that a satellite in orbit can take a pictures with a resolution of less than a foot from ranges of 150 miles or more. It's not quite reading someone's newspaper from orbit, but you can probably read car number plates.

Other sensors used to produce imagery include infra-red and video cameras, and radar systems. Television cameras are also used to transmit information via satellite to ground stations, where intelligence officers can watch the scene below in real time, as it happens.

Above: The Douglas RA-3B Skywarrior was used for reconnaissance during the Vietnam War. Usually operating from bases like Da Nang, the Skywarrior had a full camera fit. Some cameras shot infra-red film which was used to detect camouflaged targets like trucks from the heat generated by their engines.

Left: Reconnaissance at sea is similar to that on land, but places different demands on the aircraft. Currently, US Navy reconnaissance is provided by specially equipped Grumman F-14 Tomcat fighters. They carry a TARPS tactical reconnaissance pod, which enables them to do all that dedicated photo-reconnaissance planes can do, including taking pictures like this one of USS Coral Sea.

TGT: CORAL SEA	CC: US DTG: 19 JUL 85	
BE/CRS/SPD:	COORD: 3529N 07408W	
MSN: DB3012 SENSOR: KS 87 FL: 6 IN ALT: 4250 FT		
CREW: WRIGHT PARSONS	CLAS: UNCLAS	
IIR:	ENCL:	

Blackbird flying in the dead of night

A Blackbird flight was the closest thing to space travel that the US Air Force could offer to a pilot. Here, Major Duane Noll and his backseater Major Tom Veltri describe a typical mission.

Extensive pre-flight checks are necessary before a mission can take off: it takes several hours to get the aircraft ready. Once the pilot has boarded, the plane will taxi to the runway accompanied by a fleet of security and maintenance vehicles. Once at the holding point, there are still another 20 minutes of checks to go through before clearance can be given. For an aircraft that flies at three times the speed of sound, such precautions are vital

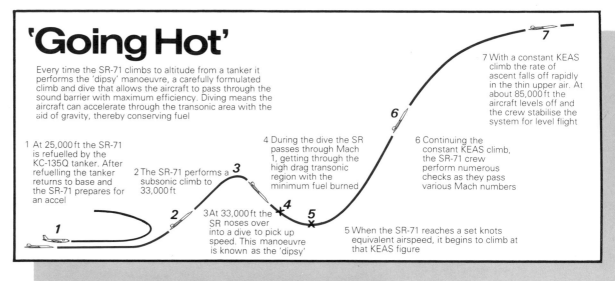

'Going Hot'

Every time the SR-71 climbs to altitude from a tanker it performs the 'dipsy' manoeuvre, a carefully formulated climb and dive that allows the aircraft to pass through the sound barrier with maximum efficiency. Diving means the aircraft can accelerate through the transonic area with the aid of gravity, thereby conserving fuel

1 At 25,000 ft the SR-71 is refuelled by the KC-135Q tanker. After refuelling the tanker returns to base and the SR-71 prepares for an accel

2 The SR-71 performs a subsonic climb to 33,000 ft

3 At 33,000 ft the SR noses over into a dive to pick up speed. This manoeuvre is known as the 'dipsy'

4 During the dive the SR passes through Mach 1, getting through the high drag transonic region with the minimum fuel burned

5 When the SR-71 reaches a set knots equivalent airspeed, it begins to climb at that KEAS figure

6 Continuing the constant KEAS climb, the SR-71 crew perform numerous checks as they pass various Mach numbers

7 With a constant KEAS climb the rate of ascent falls off rapidly in the thin upper air. At about 85,000 ft the aircraft levels off and the crew stabilise the system for level flight

To fly this kind of aircraft, at three times the speed of sound and at a cruising height of over 16 miles, takes an incredible amount of preparatory work by the countless ground staff who prepare the aircraft, compile the guidance tapes, and even help the crew dress in their very special pressure suits.

Once the pilot and the reconnaissance systems operator have climbed in, plugged in and taken off, all that support is left behind and it is up to them to fly the mission. Unlike most other flights, theirs is almost always operational. It is no-kidding stuff against no-kidding bad guys, bringing back no-kidding information.

"On the day of the mission we'll show up about three hours before the mission and go through Base Ops just like any other flight crew. After that, we go over to the PSD [Physiological Support Division] and we'll have breakfast over there. That'll be low-residue high-protein, steak and eggs or something like that. It gives you lots of energy as you won't be able to eat again for maybe six to eight hours."

While the crew are being suited up, the ground crew are warming up the engine. The SR-71 uses a special type of oil that is almost solid at room temperature. The engines are warmed up by blowing hot air through them. Meanwhile, the mission tapes are being loaded. These control the Northrop-built astro-inertial guidance system, which works by tracking 50 stars that it holds in its catalogue.

Support vehicles

Once the pre-flight checks are finished, the 107-ft aircraft taxis out onto the runway. It is accompanied by a host of support vehicles and security trucks. One car will drive the length of the runway to check for FOD – foreign object damage, bits of junk that might get sucked into the massive twin J58 turbo-ramjet engines and wreck them. Once the go is given, the SR-71 roars down the 4,000-ft runway and off into the yonder.

"We have to get the nose up to 25-30 degrees, especially on a cold day. Subsonically it's a very sturdy airplane. It handles very well. But it's not a very forgiving machine; minimum airspeeds are no-kidding minimum airspeeds. Because of the delta wing we have no indication of the stall approaching, as you get in other planes. The SR-71 just kind of falls out of the sky."

The SR-71 consumes a fair amount of fuel, and its initial task will be to rendezvous with just the first of many tankers that will have taken off hours before the SR to get in position.

"The routine is pretty basic. We have an encrypted ranging device between the two aircraft that's unjammable. This measures the distance between us, and an encrypted ADF [automatic direction finder] gauges bearings. The whole thing's done 'comms out': there's no talking between us.

Going visual

"Once he makes his turn in front of us, I keep running the rendezvous on him, up inside a mile separation. Once we go visual we just go on the boom."

From the tanker onwards the job is getting the aircraft through the sound barrier and into a supersonic climb. In order to get through the high-drag transonic area quickly, the crew perform the 'dipsy' manoeuvre before continuing the climb to operational altitude.

"We basically climb subsonically for 8,000 ft and then we'll push over into a dive for about three to four thousand, dependent on temperature. As we accelerate down we go Mach 1 and somewhere we intercept a set KEAS [Knots Equivalent Air Speed]. With the set KEAS achieved we start a constant KEAS climb. We kind of push over and take a run at this big hill we're climbing up to 80,000 ft."

The SR-71 will need to make several refuellings during its mission, each time dropping from its operational altitude of 80,000 ft down to more like 25,000 ft. Each time it does this it will repeat the procedure as it climbs away and goes 'hot', i.e. returns to its own unique altitude.

After the final refuelling the SR-71 enters the sensitive area where its sensors will work. The US Air Force will say nothing about these, except that it can cover 100,000 square miles in an hour.

Sensors

Although the SR-71 is largely unassailable at its operating height and speed, it does not overfly the target area. It uses its great altitude to gain a deep look inside the target territory, while its speed is used to map large areas in a short time, and also to provide a large measure of surprise.

The optical and radar sensors tend to be of the long-range oblique type, peering sideways from the aircraft over the target as it flies in international airspace. Black-and-white photography is still the favourite medium, and the cameras carried by the SR have large magnifications and ultra-high resolution for the best possible interpretation.

Side-looking radars are probably carried, gaining radar

Above: To cover the sort of ranges the SR-71 operated at, a fleet of KC-135Q tankers was used. The Blackbird ran on a special fuel known as JP-7, which has an extremely high flashpoint.

images deep into sensitive areas; these are particularly good at spotting military installations and large armoured formations.

Sigint (signals intelligence) gathering is the third discipline performed by the SR-71, and is considered one of great importance in today's electronic battlefield. The aircraft probably carries a secure datalink by which information can be passed in digitalised and encrypted forms for immediate interpretation.

The view from the pilot's cockpit. At 18 miles above sea level, the curvature of the Earth become apparent. At such heights, the plane was on the edge of space. In fact, its navigation system was designed around recognising star formations and constellations, not terrestrial features.

Flight profile of the SR-71

SR-71 missions were individually tailored to the specific demands of the day and the flight pattern flown would depend on many things, such as target-area position and the type of sensors to be used. This shows an example mission with two sensor runs in the target area, punctuated by refuelling.

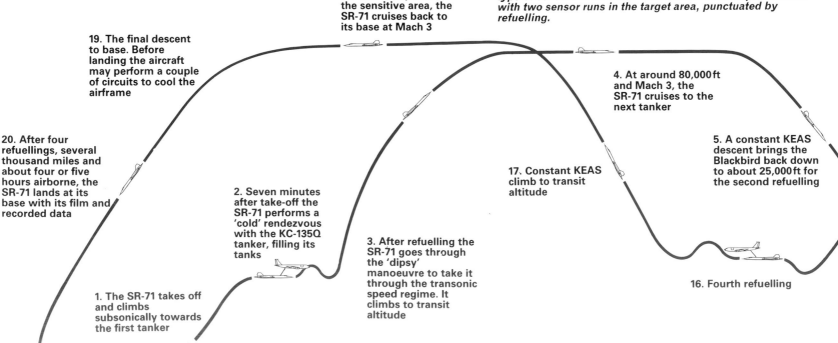

18. Well away from the sensitive area, the SR-71 cruises back to its base at Mach 3

19. The final descent to base. Before landing the aircraft may perform a couple of circuits to cool the airframe

20. After four refuellings, several thousand miles and about four or five hours airborne, the SR-71 lands at its base with its film and recorded data

1. The SR-71 takes off and climbs subsonically towards the first tanker

base

2. Seven minutes after take-off the SR-71 performs a 'cold' rendezvous with the KC-135Q tanker, filling its tanks

3. After refuelling the SR-71 goes through the 'dipsy' manoeuvre to take it through the transonic speed regime. It climbs to transit altitude

17. Constant KEAS climb to transit altitude

16. Fourth refuelling

4. At around 80,000 ft and Mach 3, the SR-71 cruises to the next tanker

5. A constant KEAS descent brings the Blackbird back down to about 25,000 ft for the second refuelling

Operating so close to hostile territory requires precise navigation to avoid embarrassing and potentially dangerous penetrations of hostile airspace. Major Veltri explains the main problem:

"Because we can only hold 35 degrees of bank, the airplane turns very slowly at supersonic speeds. It's the distance we cover: to do a 360-degree turn we're talking about a 200-mile radius.

"Having completed the mission, the SR-71 will head for home. Chances are that we will have to refuel at least once on the way. On a 'hot' rendezvous (coming from altitude) the biggest concern is starting our descent at the correct point. If we miss our descent, we're going to miss the tanker by a lot of miles, so it's important that we hit the right point. That's going to vary according to temperature and the airspeed which we've been flying at."

After the refuelling, the SR-71 will return to altitude for either a cruise back to base or for another sensor run. Sometimes the airplane is flown around for a few minutes to cool the airframe.

Once the wheels touch the ground, the pilot streams the parachute to help to slow the aircraft down. It will then taxi into its special hangar, where the long and complex bedding-down procedure takes place. The sensor data will be whisked away for immediate interpretation, and the engine oil will be drained before it goes solid. Fuel is also drained, to stop it leaking from the tanks when cold (the sealed tanks are not effective on the ground – the plane stretches over two inches in flight!). The crew undergoes a lengthy debrief, followed by a medical, and probably followed by a beer!

The SR-71 has recently been withdrawn from service, times being what they are. However, in the shady history of spyplanes there has never been, nor probably ever will be, anything quite like the 'Blackbird'.

Right: To arrest its landing run, the SR-71 streams a large parachute as well as holding its nose high.

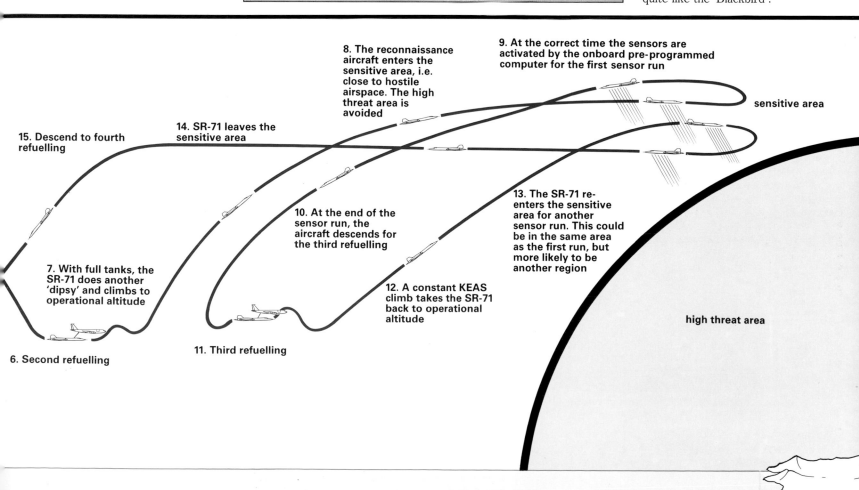

8. The reconnaissance aircraft enters the sensitive area, i.e. close to hostile airspace. The high threat area is avoided

9. At the correct time the sensors are activated by the onboard pre-programmed computer for the first sensor run

sensitive area

14. SR-71 leaves the sensitive area

15. Descend to fourth refuelling

13. The SR-71 re-enters the sensitive area for another sensor run. This could be in the same area as the first run, but more likely to be another region

10. At the end of the sensor run, the aircraft descends for the third refuelling

7. With full tanks, the SR-71 does another 'dipsy' and climbs to operational altitude

12. A constant KEAS climb takes the SR-71 back to operational altitude

11. Third refuelling

6. Second refuelling

high threat area

ALONE, UNARMED AND UNAFRAID

With spy satellites that can read the headline of a newspaper from space and the incredible SR-71 spyplane, there seems to be little need for tactical reconnaissance. Yet the Phantom RF-4 exists for just that purpose. Why?

Left: As soon as the plane touches down from its mission, technicians will be on hand to get the film away and off for developing and interpretation.

1 Cover

The RF-4 is unarmed, and so will not fly a mission without cover. On the run over there will be a top-cover escort provided by F-15s. They will either go in with the mission from the beginning or be picked up en route. F-4G 'Wild Weasels' will be used to take out radar installations, and there may be F-16s to attack ground targets and to provide air-to-air capability. Command and control for the whole operation may well be provided by an AWACS (Airborne Warning And Control System). The purpose of such a large fleet, maybe as many as 20 aircraft, is not only to protect the RF-4 but also to provide a diversion, thus hiding the true nature of the mission. If the enemy knows that a photo-recon mission has been flown, he may use that to his advantage by laying a trap.

Zweibrücken, West Germany. The base looks deserted. Not a single plane sitting on the pad. One of the massive doors of a concrete bunker – a HAS, or hardened aircraft shelter – slides back and a mighty rumbling fills the air. The effect is spooky. Even with the doors wide open, the shelter is too dark to see into. There is just a faint red glow.

Slowly the grey and green Phantom lumbers forward, the distinctive lines unbroken except for two underwing tanks each carrying 1400 litres of fuel. The aircraft taxis onto the runway, stops, waits. Suddenly a massive flame erupts from the twin J79-GE-15 turbojets. The aircraft roars down the runway and is gone.

The Phantom RF-4 has been the mainstay of the USAF's tactical photo-reconnaissance capability. The reason for sending out specially adapted aircraft over possibly heavily-held enemy territory, with no weapons to defend themselves, is simple. Flexibility.

For the commander on the ground who needs photographic information about what is ahead of him, he cannot wait for a satellite to pass over, nor would an SR-71 mission be laid on to look for a company of tanks. But to wind up a Phantom mission and get the results can take as little as two hours. To the guys on the ground, that photographic picture is worth any number of maps and sketch reports. It is the sort of information that wins battles.

1 Not all RF-4 missions will be done on quite such hot planning. More often than not, the target will have been selected some time before and the mission designed to check on developments, on whether troops are there or not there; once again, flexibility is the aim.

2 The pilot and navigator (or, to use his official title, weapons systems operator – an unusual title, given the absence of weapons), will be briefed on the mission back at base. They will prepare a flight plan using way-points selected off a map for guidance to the target area. Their visual navigation is based on terrain features such as tree patterns (remarkably constant in Europe), not cultural features such as towns, which change too quickly.

3 Most missions will be flown with a pair of RF-4s. There are two reasons for this. Firstly, if one gets shot down, the other will get the information back; secondly, although the aircraft are unarmed, they can cover each other to provide observation.

4 The RF-4s are not sent out alone. If a thing is worth taking pictures of, the chances are that it is worth defending. They will go in with cover from fighter aircraft. Ground suppression will be put in before the run, but once they go in, they're on their own.

5 The RF-4 carries 500 ft of film. The film tracks very slowly. On 10 ft of film you could record up to 16 miles of ground covered, depending on your height and speed. Missions may be flown as low as 50 ft if needed, although there is a peacetime restriction of 300 ft.

6 The choice of cameras used will depend on the end product required. An overhead view is of less use to troops on the ground than a forward oblique view that will show them what it is going to look like from their point of view. But for interpretation and mapping, an overhead view is better.

Above: The twin crew of the RF-4 need to be alert and thoroughly briefed. Unlike other spyplanes such as the SR-71 or U-2 which are to a large degree automated, the RF-4 relies on the Mk 1 eyeball for identifying the target and some fairly hairy flying to get the pictures.

2 Sensors

The RF-4 bristles with the equipment for its role. It carries flares to provide almost daytime illumination for the black-and-white cameras in night-time use and also has an infra-red reconnaissance sensor, which is not weather-dependent and will provide a result where ordinary cameras would be defeated. It also has the ability to penetrate thick woods and camouflage. There is a choice of cameras: one for low-altitude use and one for higher altitudes. Both

cameras are vertical- or sideways-mounted. In addition, there is a forward-looking camera.

For self-protection, some RF-4s will carry the ALQ-26 defensive ECM pod. This is designed to confuse and jam enemy signals and to prevent air-to-air missiles from locking onto the RF-4. There have been some models fitted with the AIM-9 'Sidewinder', but these are not now in USAF use.

The sensors and cameras of the RF-4 are: (1) Two pairs of LA-429A photoflash cartridge ejector units with 26 M112 flares of 260 million candlepower; (2) AN/AVQ-26 Pave Tack laser target designator and high-resolution detection set for ranging information and updating the navigation system; (3) AN/AAS-18 infra-red reconnaissance sensor able to detect vehicles and personnel by their heat signatures or to provide pictures at night or when obscured by smoke; (4) AN/APQ-102 SLAR with moving target indication; (5) high-altitude camera station containing vertical KA-91 camera with 18-in lens or a split of vertical KS-87s with 6- or 18-in lenses; (6) low-altitude camera station containing vertical KA-56 low-altitude panoramic camera with 3-in lens or vertical or oblique KS-87 camera with 6-, 12- or 18-in lens; (7) forward camera containing KS-87 camera with 6- or 3-in focal length lens for daytime vertical or forward oblique photography; (8) forward-looking radar in nose radome for mapping, manual terrain-following etc.

Get well point
At the end of the run the pilot banks sharply and escapes at low level.

GET WELL POINT

Sensor run
The run must be flat and steady for accurate results. The position of the aircraft will depend on threat and desired results.

TARGET

Initial point
As the RF-4 passes the initial point the navigator primes the cameras and sensors to check that they are running.

ANGLE OFF

Ingress
The route to the target is made at low level, using terrain-following to avoid detection

Climb
The first component of the manoeuvre is to climb before the target area to get up speed for the dive past it.

3 Photo run

Sophisticated types such as the SR-71 and TR-1 can get the required reconnaissance results from long stand-off distances, but the basic tactical reconnaissance aircraft has to move in close to its target to get the pictures. The target is likely to be defended, so the Phantoms have to put themselves in some danger to get the results. To survive, they use unpredictable ingress routes and fly at high speed across the target area.

4 Getting the pictures

The multiplicity of cameras and sensors on the RF-4 means that there is an equal multiplicity of methods of approach the pilot can adopt, depending on the type of sensor to be used and the nature of the anti-aircraft threat.

The RF-4C can employ a variety of techniques to photograph a target, depending on the type of sensor to be used and the nature of the anti-aircraft threat surround the target.

Against particularly 'hot' targets the Phantom would use its oblique cameras from extremely low altitude, banking to raise the camera line to the correct point. As well as keeping very low and out of the threat area, the Phantom is already banked away from the threat, making a safe egress that much quicker

Oblique photography from a large stand-off range covers a wider area at the expense of detail. The aircraft is further away from the threat source, but is also flying higher, so making it more exposed to detection and tracking

Oblique photography from lesser ranges produces good detailed imagery, but puts the Phantom inside the threat zone. However, it is flying lower so detection is more difficult

For vertical photography, another technique that can be employed is to use the oblique cameras with the aircraft in a steep bank. Although not as accurate as a straight overflight, it is less predictable and may give better imagery

Forward oblique, panoramic cameras and infra-red linescan require the RF-4C to overfly the target, which puts it into a vulnerable position. Where situations demand this overflight, the Phantom relies on its speed and a well-planned ingress route to survive

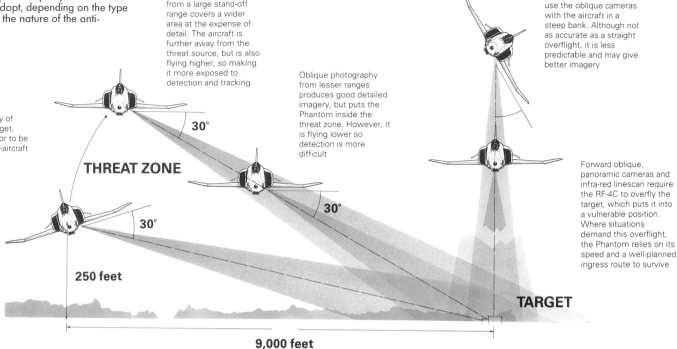

THREAT ZONE

30°

30°

30°

250 feet

9,000 feet

TARGET

5 Photographic results

There are four types of picture that the mission will produce. Infra-red linescan produces a picture based on heat rather than light. The results are similar, but may show up detail and objects that conventional film would not. Sideways oblique has the advantage that the plane need not overfly the target: this is a tactical advantage. The resulting picture may have distortion caused by the camera angle. The same is true of forward oblique. There will be a foreshortening of ground at the front of the picture, and objects in the distance will appear further away than they are in reality. Only vertical panoramic will provide an 'as-it-is' shot, but only at the centre of the image, as distortion will occur at the edges. Nevertheless, for mapping purposes this method is the most accurate.

The photographic results – the reason for the RF-4. Clockwise from the left: (1) Infra-red linescan; (2) sideways oblique; (3) forward oblique; (4) vertical panoramic. The sort of picture taken will depend on the information required.

GUNSHIP

In Vietnam, the US Air Force took Dakotas, Flying Boxcars and Hercules transports and gave them deadly teeth to turn them into fire-spitting killers that were among the most-feared weapons of the war.

When the AC-47's battery of Miniguns opened up, the noise in the cabin was ear-splitting. Gunners had to wear ear protectors to let themselves think, let alone communicate with the rest of the crew. This man would soon be ankle-deep in spent shell cases.

I f this were daylight, the Spectre would cast a big shadow over the green sea of trees. Not on this mission. It's so black out there it makes your eyeballs ache just finding where the ground ends and the sky begins. That suits us fine. The time is late 1971. We're on a night flight over Cambodia, a special (highly dangerous) operation. Our ship is an AC-130, callsign Spectre – the biggest, most deadly gunship the USAF ever used in Vietnam.

Now we're over the Trail. The guy on the TV surveillance set is watching for trucks. Contact.

The guns open up. A hit. Two, three fires. We turn the night into infra-red day as our sensors and Black Crow direction finder, tuned to Russian auto ignition systems, go to work. The beacon tracker picks up signals from a ground sensor and the computer gives directions.

Still holding the turn, we have more move-ment on the 'scope. Bang! Bang! A hit and one miss. Time to go home. Five trucks is a good night's work.

Fixed-wing gunships were the result of a combat classroom which started lessons using one old C-47, in 1964. Then, a group of pilots and crewmen went to South East Asia to prove that arming a cargo plane coming up for its 30th birthday was a great way to fight a modern war!

Circular orbit

The idea was not new. In 1927 a pilot had found that a D.H.4 biplane could, flying a cir-cular, 'pylon turn' course, hit a small ground target with a side-firing machine-gun.

Although successful, the idea was shelved until the 1960s. It was found that by holding a C-47 in a bank to port and using a cockpit sight, side-firing guns could hit a small target with devastating accuracy while maintaining a

An AC-130 gunship can put a round into every square foot of a football field in just over 60 seconds.

Firing for accuracy

It was found that to be effective the AC-47 needed to maintain a circular orbit around the target, with the pilot holding the aircraft in a bank. This enabled the gunners to saturate a point area on the ground. If the aircraft is flown in a circular path at a given height the weapons will be consistently on target. Initially pilots used the classic 3-4-5 triangle to calculate the angle; this was later replaced by fire control computers.

Early on, the AC-47 was fitted with a battery of standard machine-guns. These often jammed or overheated from the necessary high volume of rounds, so the more efficient, rotary-barrel General Electric Minigun became the answer to the gunship armament requirement. And it didn't need much modification to fit.

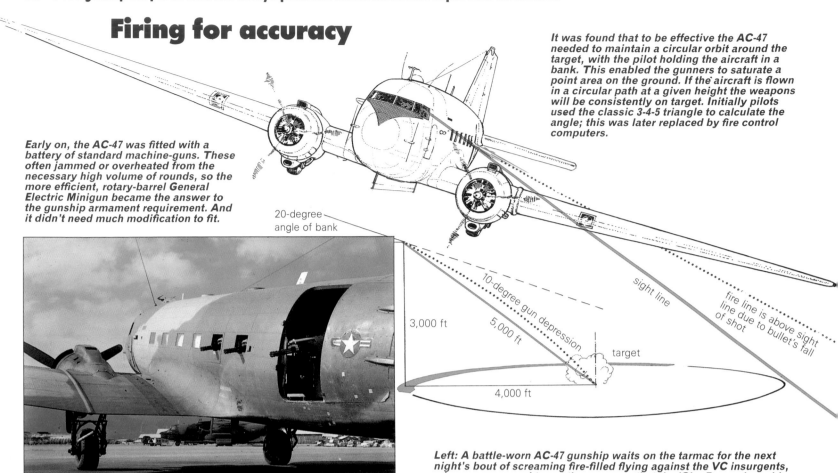

20-degree angle of bank

10-degree gun depression

sight line

fire line is above sight line due to bullet's fall of shot

3,000 ft

5,000 ft

target

4,000 ft

Left: A battle-worn AC-47 gunship waits on the tarmac for the next night's bout of screaming fire-filled flying against the VC insurgents, who never seemed to get the message that the 'Sky Dragon' would burn them up wherever he found them. This is the standard three-Minigun battery of the early gunship.

circular orbit. With a modern revolving-barrel Minigun firing 6,000 rounds a minute, a four-second burst would put 400 bullets in a 31-foot diameter circle.

Someone thought the rain of fire looked like the hot breath of a dragon. 'Puff the Magic Dragon' was then a popular song, so Puff became the gunship callsign.

Early gunships lacked modern weapons. Engineers simply drilled holes in the C-47's door and windows for 0.3 calibre machine-guns to fire through. They weren't too reliable and often jammed – but they proved the gunship theory.

With just one aircraft, the Puff crews were kept very busy. In a war that was really hundreds of localised battles, commanders liked the pinpoint accuracy of Puff. Often they'd scream for gunship support rather than fighter bomber support. Clearly more AC-47s were needed – and fast.

In 1965 a new squadron, the 4th Air Commando, began training, and 20 C-47s were converted to gunships. The 4th ACS distributed its aircraft and crews throughout South Vietnam, on call to get ground forces out of trouble around the clock. At bases like Da Nang, Pleiku, Bien Hoa and Binh Tuy, the

telephones rang constantly in the Puff operations shack.

After a brief, near-suicidal try at interdicting the Ho Chi Minh Trail, where groundfire was deadly, the AC-47s stayed South. The 4th ACS became part of the 14th Special Operations Wing, widely known as the Antique Wing due to most of its aircraft being older than the men who flew them!

Decoy C-47

Gunships, which took the callsign Spooky in 1966, often worked in pairs. A favourite trick was to send out a standard C-47 fitted with

GUNSHIP Reference File

83
Douglas AC-47 'Spooky'

USA

During the Vietnam War the US Air Force soon became convinced that a gunship aeroplane, able to pour down massive concentrations of fire on comparatively small areas of ground where an enemy might be hiding, could prove a decisive weapon.

The first such aeroplane was the 'Gunship I' development of the C-47, initially designated FC-47D and then **AC-47D 'Spooky'**. This was a comparatively simple development of the basic transport aeroplane with three MXU-470/A Minigun multi-barrel machine-guns and 21,000 rounds of ammunition. The guns were located on the gunship's port side (in the fifth and sixth windows and the cargo door), and the operational tactic was a steady left-

hand orbit round the target area so that the pilot could aim and fire the weapons, whose ammunition was replenished by armourers who also launched flares in nocturnal operations.

Some 32 C-47Ds were converted to AC-47D standard, and these were operated from November 1965 by the 4th Air Commando Squadron, which was later divided into the 4th and 14th Air Commando (later Special Operations) Squadrons. The AC-47D was phased out of US service in December 1968, surviving aircraft being passed to the South Vietnamese and Laotian air forces.

Specification
Douglas AC-47D 'Spooky'
Type: six/seven-seat aerial gunship
Powerplant: two 895-kW (1,200-hp) Pratt & Whitney R-1830-92 piston engines
Performance: maximum speed 370 km/h (230 mph); range 2575 km

(1,600 miles)
Dimensions: span 29.11 m (95 ft 6 in); length 19.43 m (63 ft 9 in)
Weights: empty not revealed; maximum take-off 11793 kg (26,000 lb)
Armament: three 7.62-mm (0.3-in) Miniguns
Users: Laos, South Vietnam and USA

loudspeakers. This would orbit and implore the VC not to fire at it or great wrath would befall them. When the call was ignored, a blacked-out Spooky, invisible above the first one, would open fire. The last thing many an enemy soldier heard were the words, 'I told you so' echoing out of the night sky . . .

By 1967 a second squadron, the 3rd SOS, was in Vietnam. The AC-47s soldiered on for two more years until the AC-119 largely replaced it. The Flying Boxcar conversion got

Below: A time exposure photograph makes the streams of gunship fire in the sky over a target look like fireworks. Every line represents a stream of shells from Miniguns.

into service before the Herc, although the C-130 was the true Spooky follow-on.

Among the problems with the AC-47 was that it was slow, old, small and not very plentiful. The C-130 solved all these problems in one airframe big enough for the black boxes and sensor equipment to find Charlie wherever he hid, night or day.

Truck-hunting

With one converted C-130A, Spectre went into combat. Armed with four 7.62-mm Miniguns and four 20-mm Gatling cannon, plus a Starlite Scope, searchlight and computer to work out the target co-ordinates, the Her-

84

Lockheed AP-2H Neptune

USA

It is a relatively little-known fact that the US Navy was also involved in the operation of aerial gunships during the Vietnam War. The main navy units involved were the Naval Air Test Center's 'Project TRIM' detachment at Cam Ranh Bay and other bases from late 1967, and Heavy Attack Squadron 21 based at Cam Ranh Bay for a few months from September 1968. These units operated mainly over the Mekong River delta on interdiction work until VAH-21 was disbanded in March 1969.

The aircraft involved were four P-2Hs modified to **AP-2H Neptune** standard with the E-Systems TRIM (Trails & Roads Interdiction, Multi-sensor) package. Little has been revealed about this target-acquisition package, but it

probably included a FLIR, low-light-level TV and terrain-avoidance radar. The aircraft were also adapted for nocturnal operations with flame-dampers on the exhausts of the piston engines, and 'hush-kits' on the auxiliary turbojets.

The armament described below (which included two rear-firing 20-mm cannon for the engagement of targets that had been overflown) could also be supplemented by pintle-mounted 7.62-mm (0.3-in) M60 machine-guns located on each beam in the removable rear-fuselage windows.

Specification
Lockheed AP-2H Neptune
Type: multi-seat aerial gunship
Powerplant: two 2610-kW (3,500-hp)

Wright R-3350-32W Turbo-Compound piston engines and two 1542-kg (3,400-lb) thrust Westinghouse J34-WE-32W turbojets
Performance: maximum speed 648 km/h (403 mph); range 3450 km (2,200 miles)
Dimensions: span 31.65 m (103 ft

10 in); length 27.94 m (91 ft 8 in)
Weights: empty not revealed; maximum take-off 36240 kg (79,895 lb)
Armament: six 20-mm M24 cannon, two SUU-11B/A pods each carrying one 7.62-mm (0.3-in) Minigun, and up to four pods for a maximum of 76 70-mm (2.75-in) rockets

'Fabulous Four-Engined Fighter' was the affectionate nick-name that AC-130 gunship crews gave their aircraft. These lethal Hercs were the logical follow-on to the Dakota, and they ended up carrying the biggest aerial gun of the war.

85
Fairchild NC-123K 'Black Spot'

USA

Another little-known participant in the interdiction campaign during the Vietnam War was the **NC-123K 'Black Spot'** version of the C-123K Provider light tactical transport. Only two such conversions were made, and these operated with the 606th Air Commando Squadron based at Nakhon Phanom Air Base in Thailand between 1968 and 1971.

The NC-123K featured an advanced sensor package second only to that of the AC-130A/E in sophistication, the nose being revised with a large radome above a substantial sensor turret. The package included forward-looking search radar, a FLIR, a low-light-level TV and a laser rangefinder, while the type also accommodated an advanced

navigation system and a computer-controlled release system for the type's disposable load of anti-vehicle and anti-personnel bomblets.

The two aircraft were used for nocturnal interdiction over the Ho Chi Minh Trail, and though they were quite successful they lacked the capabilities and survivability of the AC-130 variants and thus enjoyed only a limited career. After storage in the USA, the aircraft were restored to light transport configuration and transferred to Thailand.

Specification
Fairchild NC-123K 'Black Spot'
Type: multi-seat night interdictor

Powerplant: two 1864-kW (2,500-hp) Pratt & Whitney R-2800-99W piston engines and two 1293-kg (2,850-lb) thrust General Electric J85-GE-17 turbojets
Performance: maximum speed 367 km/h (228 mph); range 1665 km (1,035 miles)

Dimensions: span 33.53 m (110 ft 0 in); length 23.24 m (76 ft 3 in)
Weights: empty not revealed; maximum take-off 27216 kg (60,000 lb)
Armament: an unrevealed weight of bomblets
User: USA

86
Fairchild AU-23A Peacemaker

USA

In 1971 the USA was becoming increasingly involved in the 'Vietnamisation' of the Vietnam War in a programme designed to make South Vietnam better able to shoulder the burden of its own defence so that American forces could be pulled out. The programme envisaged, amongst other things, the development of 'mini-gunships' for South Vietnamese use, and one of the types considered was a STOL utility transport based on the Pilatus Turbo-Porter.

Though trials in 1972 at Eglin AFB, Florida, convinced most US Air Force officers that the **AU-23A Peacemaker** was too small and light for effective development into an aerial gunship, orders were placed late in the

year for 15 such machines. The type was fitted with four underwing hardpoints for light drop loads and rocket-launcher pods, but the gunship capability was vested in a 20-mm three-barrel located in the cabin to fire through the door with the aid of a TVS-5 night vision sight.

Testing in 1972 was delayed by a number of problems, but the AU-23A was finally cleared for operations. Effectiveness and survivability were rated marginal, and the aircraft were placed in storage for a time before 13 finally reached the Thai air force.

Specification
Fairchild AU-23A Peacemaker
Type: three/four-seat aerial gunship

Powerplant: one 496-kW (665-shp) Garrett-AiResearch TPE331-1-101F turboprop
Performance: maximum speed 280 km/h (174 mph); range 900 km (558 miles)
Dimensions: span 15.14 m (49 ft 8 in); length 11.23 m (36 ft 10 in)

Weights: empty not revealed; maximum take-off 2767 kg (6,100 lb)
Armament: one 20-mm XM197 cannon and up to 636 kg (1,400 lb) of disposable stores carried under the wings
User: Thailand

cules could now go truck hunting along the Trail. On the first mission, six trucks were blasted. The USAF ordered more Spectres.

As insurance, because the Trail was still one of the hottest spots in South East Asia, Spectres usually had a shotgun guard of F-4s. Meanwhile the AC-119 went into action to fill any gap left after AC-47 phase-out.

Two models

There were two AC-119 gunships, callsign Shadow. The G model, armed with four Miniguns, a xenon light, night observation sight and flare launcher, was a support ship while the K model, with two pod-mounted J85 jet engines, was a dedicated truck killer. The AC-119K, often known as 'Stinger', had two more guns, terrain-following and search radar, FLIR – Forward-Looking Infra-Red – and other magic tracking devices.

Entering combat in 1968 with the 14th SOW at Na Trang, two squadrons of Shadows flew every sort of mission, day and night, until late 1971.

Surprise package

By 1968, there were eight AC-130s, all of them slightly different. Aircraft No 9 was the prototype for the Surprise Package AC-130.

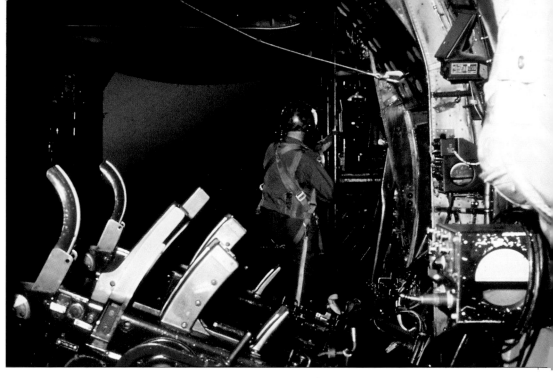

Above: In the belly of the Spectre, the breeches of two of the 40-mm cannon can be seen in the foreground and, beyond, the open rear loading ramp. The AC-130E was aptly named 'Surprise Package'.

That package consisted of a FLIR, an LLLTV – Low Light Level Television camera – beacon tracking, side-looking radar, laser designator and a video bomb damage recorder. A digital fire control computer worked out the best attack profiles. To make room for the equipment, two Miniguns were taken out and replaced by two 40-mm Bofors guns.

For the enemy, worse was to come. The success of the early Spectres led to the far-

---

87
Helio AU-24A Stallion

USA

The competitor evaluated by the US Air Force against the Fairchild AU-23A in the 'Credible Chase' programme to provide the South Vietnamese air force with a simply maintained and easily operated 'mini-gunship' was the **AU-24A Stallion**, a development of the civilian Stallion Model H-550A. This was a utility light transport with excellent STOL capability, and 15 evaluation aircraft were ordered late in 1971.

For its military role the Stallion was provided with five hardpoints (two under each wing and one under the fuselage) as well as provision in the cabin for a side-firing 20-mm three-barrel cannon complete with its ammunition container and TVS-5 night

vision sight. Evaluation of the AU-24A got under way in April 1972, and despite several delays was completed by May of the same year.

Like the AU-23A, the AU-24A was judged to have only marginal capability and problematical survivability, so all 15 aircraft were relegated to outdoor storage at Davis-Monthan AFB, Arizona, at the end of the test programme. However, 14 of the aircraft were eventually delivered to the Cambodian air force.

Specification
Helio AU-24A Stallion
Type: three/four-seat aerial gunship
Powerplant: one 507-kW (680-shp) Pratt & Whitney Canada PT6A-27

turboprop
Performance: maximum speed 348 km/h (216 mph); range 716 km (445 miles)
Dimensions: span 12.5 m (41 ft 0 in); length 12.07 m (39 ft 7 in)
Weights: empty not revealed; maximum take-off 2857 kg (6,300 lb)

Armament: one 20-mm XM197 cannon and up to 1043 kg (2,300 lb) of disposable stores carried externally
User: Cambodia

88
Martin B-57G

USA

To provide a high-quality night interdiction capability against the Ho Chi Minh Trail, 16 B-57B night intruders were converted into **B-57G** intruders with a self-contained night attack package in a drastically revised, bulbous nose. Developed by Westinghouse, the package included forward-looking search radar, a FLIR, a low-light-level TV and a laser ranger and marked-target seeker.

Eleven such aircraft were allocated to the 13th Bomb Squadron at Ubon Air Base, Thailand, from September 1970, and in the 'Tropic Moon III' campaign proved highly successful. Once detected and identified by the sensors, the target was ranged and illuminated by the laser system so that a 227-kg

(500-lb) guided bomb of the Paveway I series could home onto it with great accuracy. With this package the B-57 in its twilight years finally fulfilled the night intruder promise that had so long been denied by lack of adequate target-acquisition capability.

In the 'Pave Gat' programme, at least one B-57G was revised with a 20-mm XM197 three-barrel cannon in a trainable ventral mounting (in the bomb bay area) for evaluation as an aerial gunship. The trials were generally successful, but the type was not used operationally in Vietnam.

Specification
Martin B-57G
Type: two-seat night intruder and

interdictor
Powerplant: two 3266-kg (7,500-lb) thrust Wright J65-W-5 turbojets
Performance: maximum speed 937 km/h (582 mph); range 3701 km (2,300 miles)
Dimensions: span 19.51 m (64 ft 0 in); length 19.96 m (65 ft 6 in) for B-57B

Weights: empty not revealed; maximum take-off 24948 kg (55,000 lb)
Armament: up to 2722 kg (6,000 lb) of bombs carried internally and up to 16 127-mm (5-in) rockets carried under the wings
User: USA

Above: **Grenada was the AC-130's second war, and it did well again, spearheading the US invasion force and protecting unarmed transport Hercs by suppressing ground fire.**

Below: **American ground troops establish control during the invasion of Panama in December 1989. They can call on gunship support directly and often use their firepower to sanitise enemy strongpoints. Note the white armbands on the left arms of the soldiers: these enabled the gunships above, using infra-red sights, to identify friendly troops during nighttime operations.**

reaching Pave Pronto programme, followed by the Pave Spectre AC-130E and H models, operated by the 16th SOS.

Tank targets

The last AC-130s packed a 105-mm howitzer to stand off, out of ground fire range and shoot up trucks with 44-lb shells. All Pave Spectre Hercs had the howitzer and as AC-130Hs, they did sterling work during the 1972 spring invasion of South Vietnam, when the targets were often tanks. Working with F-4s, the Spectres used their laser illuminators to guide smart bombs.

When the 16th SOS went home in 1975, it was not the end of the story. So well had gunships performed that the Air Force maintained them for later use in the Grenada invasion and Central American operations.

Below: **Smoke erupts from a gunship-hit target in central Panama during the invasion. Gunships are ideal weapons for use in surgical strikes in towns and cities, where the firepower can be directed with pinpoint accuracy.**

Big Gunships

The third of the USAF gunships based on transport aircraft, the AC-119 'Shadow' was introduced to Vietnam combat in 1968 and was intended to fill any gap left by AC-47 phase-out. Along with the AC-130, the AC-119 did sterling work as a gunship.

89
USA

Fairchild AC-119G 'Shadow' and AC-119K 'Stinger'

The AC-47D's successor in US Air Force service was the AC-119 'Gunship III' conversion of the C-119 Flying Boxcar transport. The first version was the **AC-119G 'Shadow'** that was evolved in 1967 on the basis of the C-119G with a powerplant of two radial piston engines. This variant was designed for the 'in-country' fire support role, and was equipped along the port side of the central nacelle with a Night Observation Sight (NOS), four Minigun multi-barrel machine-guns, and an AVQ-8 searchlight: 26 conversions were made.

Last and best of the US gunships, the AC-130 had an airframe large enough to pack in all the latest late-1960s techno-surveillance devices plus awesome gunpower.

90
USA

Lockheed AC-130A 'Plain Jane', AC-130A 'Pave Pronto' and AC-130E/H 'Pave Spectre'3

The most important gunships of the Vietnam War were undoubtedly the AC-130 conversions of the C-130 Hercules tactical transport. These 'Gunship II' types began with a single 1967 conversion of a C-130A to **AC-130A** standard with four Vulcan multi-barrel cannon and four Minigun multi-barrel machine-guns supported by multiple sensors (Night Observation Sight, low-light-level TV and laser rangefinder in the forward port-side door, and an APQ-133 beacon-

# of Vietnam

The more advanced **AC-119K 'Stinger'** for 'out-country' interdiction of the Ho Chi Minh Trail had additional power as well as greater firepower and more advanced sensors in the form (nose to tail) of an AAD-4 FLIR, a NOS, a Vulcan six-barrel cannon, four Miniguns, a Vulcan cannon, an APQ-133 beacon tracking radar and a searchlight: again, 26 conversions were made.

The type reached Vietnam in January 1969 in the hands of the 71st Special Operations Squadron, but the two primary operators were the 17th and 18th SOSs with the AC-119G and AC-119K respectively. The types were phased out of service in September 1971 and December 1972 respectively, surviving aircraft being passed to the South Vietnamese air force.

Used as a transport in the Korean war, the C-119's main Vietnam war role was the gunship mission. With 20-mm and 7.62-mm guns, it flew in interdictor and fire support roles.

Specification
Fairchild AC-119K 'Stinger'
Type: multi-seat aerial gunship
Powerplant: two 2525-kW (3,400-hp) Wright R-23350-89W piston engines and two 1293-kg (2,850-lb) thrust General Electric J85-GE-17 turbojets
Performance: maximum speed 402 km/h (250 mph); range 3186 km (1,980 miles)
Dimensions: span 33.3 m (109 ft 3 in); length 26.36 m (86 ft 6 in)
Weights: empty 26436 kg (58,282 lb); maximum take-off 36469 kg (80,000 lb)
Armament: two 20-mm cannon and four 7.62-mm (0.3-in) Miniguns
Users: South Vietnam and USA

Basic prop power of the AC-119 was two Wright R-3350 radials. The G model had a single J85 turbojet in a pod under each wing, giving it four-engined safety on combat missions.

To enable the AC-119 to find its often elusive enemy, it was fitted with a range of sensors to find its main truck targets.

If the target proved very elusive, the AC-119 had a 'black light' xenon searchlight that could turn darkness into electronic day for Gunners to see and destroy.

---

tracking radar in the rear port-side door). Vietnamese evaluation late in 1967 was so successful that seven JC-130A missile-tracking aircraft were modified to the same **'Plain Jane'** standard, and these served with the 16th Special Operations Squadron from late 1968.

The concept was taken a step further in the nine **'Pave Pronto'** aircraft: these had an armament of two Miniguns, two Vulcans and two 40-mm Bofors guns, while the sensors were augmented by an ASD-5 ignition detector, AAD-7 FLIR, AVQ-17 searchlight and APQ-150 beacon-tracking radar.

The ultimate Vietnamese War gunships were the 11 **AC-130E** gunships with one of the 40-mm guns replaced by a 105-mm (4.13-in) howitzer. The aircraft entered service from 1971 and proved truly devastating, and in 1973 became **AC-130H** aircraft when fitted with more powerful T56-A-15 turboprops.

With its four Allison turboprops giving good power output and reliability, the C-130 was the ideal gunship. It also had better range than either the Spooky or Shadow types.

Specification
Lockheed AC-130E 'Pave Spectre'
Type: multi-seat aerial gunship
Powerplant: four 3020-kW (4,050-eshp) Allison T56-A-7 turboprops
Performance: maximum speed 612 km/h (380 mph); endurance 5 hours
Dimensions: span 40.41 m (132 ft 7 in); length 29.79 m (97 ft 9 in)
Weights: empty 33063 kg (72,892 lb); maximum take-off 70307 kg (155,000 lb)
Armament: one 105-mm (4.13-in) howitzer, one 40-mm Bofors gun, two 20-mm Vulcan cannon and two 7.62-mm (0.3-in) Miniguns
User: USA

Gun arming and firing followed a set sequence of actions, after detection by the sensors and positive identification. The pilot always set up the target and ordered the gunners to fire.

The massive upsweep of the Hercules' rear fuselage enabled a wide ramp door to extend for vehicles to drive in. Gunships had a blister in the ramp floor to watch targets through.

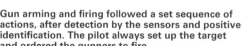

Although most Vietnam gunships had black undersides, a new colour, 'gunship grey', was actually found to blend better with the sky when the aircraft was seen from below.

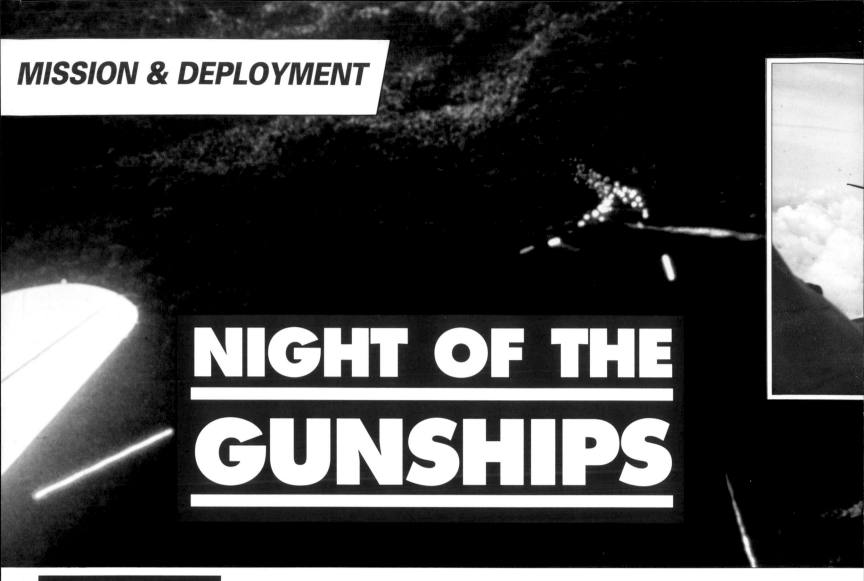

NIGHT OF THE GUNSHIPS

When it came to interdicting the Ho Chi Minh Trail, transport conversion gunships were fast enough to stay out of trouble, but could throttle back to keep a target in sight.

The modern gunship is a grey ghost of an aircraft, packed with sophisticated target detection and acquisition systems and armed to the teeth. It has been used to great effect in recent US military operations in central America, most notably during the invasions of Grenada and Panama. But it was as a black-painted creature of the South East Asian night that the gunship made its name.

It was often said that the Vietnam night belonged to Charlie. This was certainly true in places, but the Viet Cong soon found that when Spooky, Shadow or Spectre was around, then hails of leaden death from the skies meant that it was really the night of the gunship.

Snarling weapons

Gunships were unlikely candidates for the role as most effective weapon of the war, but these converted cargo planes saved the lives of countless ordinary grunts. From the epic battle for Khe Sanh through to countless individual actions in support of seemingly hopelessly cut-off patrols, gunships split the night with the characteristic snarl of their guns. And wherever the fountain of light created by their tracer shells touched down, then the enemy was taking a beating.

Gunship theory called for flying an aeroplane with side-firing guns in a turn so as to bring the guns to bear on a fixed point of the ground. It was not a system for use in high-threat environments, but for the counter-insurgency war in Vietnam it was ideal.

Spooky

The FC-47 conversion of the venerable C-47 proved remarkably successful at hosing down Viet Cong insurgents attacking US installations. Known as 'Spooky', or 'Puff the Magic Dragon', its designation was changed to AC-47 when fighter pilots complained at sharing a designation with a converted cargo bird.

By the 1970s, however, the war had grown considerably beyond counter-insurgency. A flood of men and material came pouring down the Ho Chi Minh Trail. The AC-47 did not have what it took to to deal with such targets, so more capable platforms were developed. Spooky was followed in its turn by conversions of the C-119 and the C-130 Hercules, which became known as Spectre and was the definitive gunship.

Below: The deadly hot breath of Spooky roars out over an enemy target in Vietnam. The AC-47 had few electronic detection aids, so flares were widely used to turn night into lethal daylight.

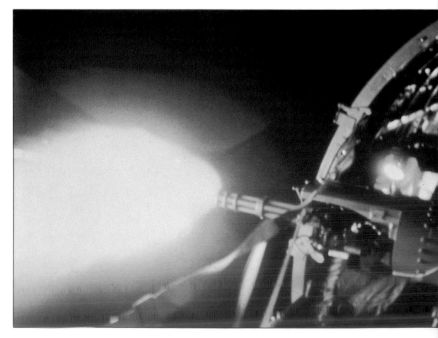

Left: A Spooky AC-47 gunship is snapped from a window of a following aircraft en route to a target in Vietnam.

Right: A South Vietnamese air force AC-119 blazes away during the 1975 invasion.

Below: Shadowing the camera ship, an AC-119 shows off its snout on the way to a rendezvous with the enemy. One of the Vulcan barrels can be seen poking out of the right-hand side of the fuselage.

Spooky

The old 'Gooney Bird' had all the attributes needed for a gunship. It was large enough to carry the weight of three 7.62-mm Miniguns and their ammunition, and still give the gun crews room to work. It could fly slowly, which was an essential ability when you had to spend a lot of time loitering about a target area. It also had long endurance. It was vulnerable to ground fire, but no more than any of the helicopters serving in Vietnam in their thousands. The gunships became known as 'Spooky' in 1966 after the callsign of the 4th AC Squadron, the first operational squadron in Vietnam.

Search and Destroy

The task of the gunship is to annihilate the enemy, either while he is on the move or when he is attacking friendly troops.

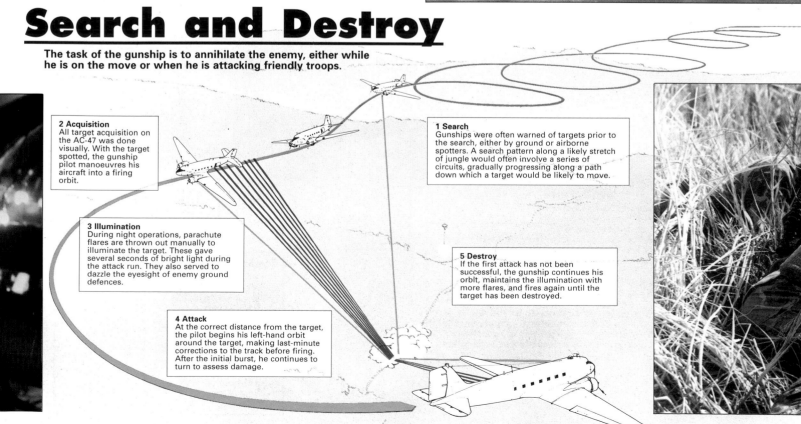

2 Acquisition
All target acquisition on the AC-47 was done visually. With the target spotted, the gunship pilot manoeuvres his aircraft into a firing orbit.

1 Search
Gunships were often warned of targets prior to the search, either by ground or airborne spotters. A search pattern along a likely stretch of jungle would often involve a series of circuits, gradually progressing along a path down which a target would be likely to move.

3 Illumination
During night operations, parachute flares are thrown out manually to illuminate the target. These gave several seconds of bright light during the attack run. They also served to dazzle the eyesight of enemy ground defences.

5 Destroy
If the first attack has not been successful, the gunship continues his orbit, maintains the illumination with more flares, and fires again until the target has been destroyed.

4 Attack
At the correct distance from the target, the pilot begins his left-hand orbit around the target, making last-minute corrections to the track before firing. After the initial burst, he continues to turn to assess damage.

Stinger and Shadow

Although Spooky was making a supreme contribution to the Vietnam War, the C-47's low-set wing meant that guns had to be mounted aft, where the fuselage is least capacious. The first choice of replacement was the C-130 Hercules, but most of these magnificent ships were needed as airlifters. As an interim measure the Fairchild C-119 was selected and adapted, and became known as Shadow (AC-119G) or Stinger (the jet-boosted AC-119K). This last was armed with a pair of powerful multi-barrelled 20-mm cannon in addition to three 7.62-mm Miniguns.

Far left: A SEAL goes in on a mission in Rung Sat in 1967 while gunships keep the enemy's heads down. Left: A column of North Vietnamese guerrillas. The camouflage carried here was very effective, and often hid heavy AAA.

EYE WITNESS

"About two in the morning, a Shadow gunship appeared overhead. Armed with four Miniguns and a giant searchlight, the AC-119G came in from the north-west and swept the draw below 1st Platoon's position with Minigun fire, a 24,000-round a minute torrent that stripped the trees in its path almost bare of leaves and cut a swathe through the jungle thirty metres wide. For the next forty minutes, the Shadow made repeated runs up and down the draw. When its ordnance was finally expended, the plane turned on its searchlight, holding the edge of the beam just below 1st Platoon's perimeter. Two Cobra gunships came in next, dived in under the light and for the next fifteen minutes fired up the draw with more Minigun fire."

**Mortarman Samuel Zaffiri,
1st Infantry Division, Vietnam**

Pow

The A
four A
turbop
some
horse
gunsh
of mo
a max
4000
the bi
hours

EYE WITNESS

"I was blessed with a good crew and what I consider to be the finest airplane ever built. Although the AC-130s we flew were the first ones ever built, they were sturdy and state-of-the-art weapons systems. I believe that the few AC-130 aircraft assigned to the 16th Special Ops Squadron contributed immeasurably to our efforts in South East Asia. We received little recognition and, when compared to other flying units, very little reward. All of our missions were over Laos, since President Johnson's prohibition of North Vietnamese airspace was on at that time. This allowed the North Vietnamese to bring a good part of their anti-aircraft artillery into Laos, which they did. It was not unusual to receive 300-500 rounds of AAA on one four-hour mission."

**Lt Colonel William Schwehm,
CO, Spectre crew, 16th SOS**

Above: Pointing ominously at the paddy fields below, the barrels of the twin 40-mm cannon fitted in the aptly-named 'Surprise Package' AC-130 await the order to fire on an unsuspecting enemy column. The beauty of Spectre was that it was not easy for the enemy to distinguish it from a standard transport Hercules.

Spectre Surprise

Lockheed's 'Fabulous Four-Engined Fighter' first saw the light of day in 1967 when an early C-130 Hercules was converted to gunship configuration. Tests of the 'Super Spook' in Vietnam showed that the four 20-mm cannon and four 7.62-mm Miniguns were much more effective than the AC-47, but it was not until 1969 that the first squadron made it to the war zone. Given the codename 'Spectre', and fitted with the best night vision and sensor gear available, the AC-130 was the definitive gunship.

When the US Air Force brought the mighty AC-130 Hercules gunship into operational service in May 1969, it devised one of the most effective truck-killing weapons of the Vietnam War. Considering that a great deal of the US effort was aimed at slowing – and preferably stopping – the flow of supplies down the Ho Chi Minh Trail to arm the Viet Cong and North Vietnamese Army in the South, the gunship concept was ingenious.

A typical gunship mission took place in March 1972, by which

time the AC-130s were based at Ubon, Thailand, sharing the dispersals with the F-4 Phantoms of the 8th TFW, with which the crews often worked in 'hunter-killer' teams.

Take-off time for the gunship was just after 8 p.m. It took about an hour and 20 minutes for the Spectre to reach its operational area.

As the big aircraft drones over the border into Laos, powerful sensors feel out invisibly into the night, striving to pick up signs of

movement along the network of roads and tracks, the arteries that fed the war. Apart from the occasional stab of headlights as North Vietnamese drivers pulled their vehicles through a particularly tough corner, you could fly over the Trail at night in a normal aircraft and see absolutely nothing.

With the Spectre having reached a likely spot, the operators of the ship's highly specialised electronics hunch over their displays. They sit in 'the

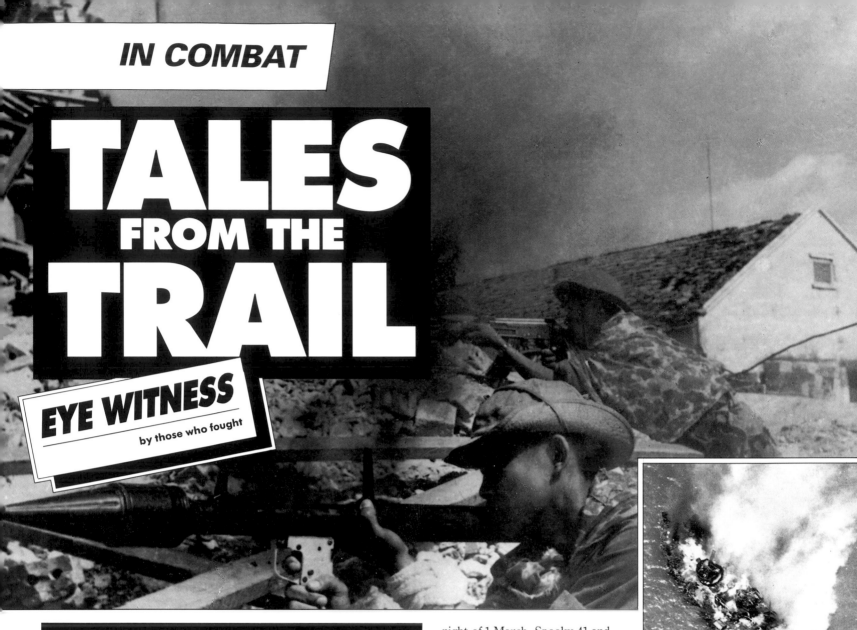

TALES FROM THE TRAIL

EYE WITNESS
by those who fought

During the Tet offensive of 1968, the AC-47 dealt savage blows against the Viet Cong. To the troops in camps all over Vietnam, Spooky became their true 'Guardian Angel'.

Spooky on the Line

The enemy's Tet offensive dictated an almost complete commitment of air power. Spooky gunships were hard-pressed to keep up with demands on them. On several occasions AC-47s on airborne alert were able to instantly pinpoint rocket and mortar positions firing on friendly installations. For example, as the offensive began, the 4th Air Commando Squadron AC-47s and crews were sent from Nha Trang and Phu Cat to Da Nang to bolster security in that often hit area. On the night of 3/4 March the Viet Cong and North Vietnamese assaulted 12 separate locations in the Da Nang tactical area of operations but did not strike the air base. At the time, Spooky 11 and Spooky 12 were flying airborne combat patrols over Da Nang and its helicopter satellite field, Marble Mountain. Minutes after the enemy attacked south-west of the main base, Spooky 11 engaged the site firing the rockets. Secondary explosions erupted. The next day, ground parties came upon unused rocket rounds indicating a premature end of the enemy attack.

Two other operations underscored the advantages of the Spooky gunships in 1968. The night of 1 March, Spooky 41 and Spooky 42 attacked a 700-ton munition trawler at Bai Cay Bay, 11 miles north of the gunships' base at Nha Trang. The trawler was exchanging fire with US and Vietnamese gunboats. In the words of Spooky 41's commander, Lt Col Richard C. Lothrop:

"We had been firing on the ship and it had run aground about 20 yards from the shore. It began burning. In a few minutes, the intensity of the fire had greatly increased. Then it just blew up. It was a spectacular explosion. . . A fireball went 1,000 feet into the air. It was obviously a load of munitions."

Lt Col Robert C. Dillon, commander of Spooky 42 (which relieved Spooky 41), reported:

"There was a large secondary explosion when we fired on the tree line just north of the beach area where the ship was grounded. Ten minutes later we were working over an area south-west of the burning ship when we caused another secondary explosion about 180 feet up the side of a hill."

Together, Spooky 11 and Spooky 42 expended more than 38,000 rounds while on the scene from 0130 to 0700. They were credited with sinking one ship and destroying tons of enemy munitions.

Call for help

The second Spooky operation occurred in western Quang Duc Province. It was in defence of a compound at Duc Lap consisting of MACV subsector headquarters,

Below: An AC-47 banks as the pilot sights the target and his gunners in the back crank out their continuous streams of Minigun fire. This was a relatively cheap way to cause harm to the enemy in a difficult jungle environment that gave him most of the advantages.

Left: When the Viet Cong burst into the suburbs of Saigon early in 1968, the war in Vietnam took a dramatic turn. Although squads of troops like these were wiped out, and gunships mopped up many danger areas, the conflict changed from then on.

Left: Even floating targets like a Vietnamese patrol boat were gunship fodder – anything the enemy used to move supplies was attacked by the prowling cargo aircraft. Recon photos like this were vital to get a big picture of where the enemy was and what his next move might be.

Left: A Minigun spits fire across the Asian plain as an AC-47 gunship opens up on suspected VC positions in the Mekong Delta in 1966.

Civilian Irregular Defense Group camp, and outposts. The Viet Cong and North Vietnamese opened up on the compound at 0105 on 23 August. Firing of rockets and mortars was instantly followed by a sapper attack on key positions. US Army helicopters arrived within 30 minutes of a call for air support. Two Spookies from Nha Trang and Pleiku joined the action 15 minutes later.

At once they illuminated the area and raked the defence perimeters with Minigun fire. Enemy sappers cut through extensive wire emplacements and several fire fights broke out within the compound. Eight American advisors, six wounded, abandoned their burning bunker at 0700 to take up positions on the north-east defence perimeter. The gunships experienced heavy

automatic fire from at least 10 anti-aircraft sites spotted around the embattled area. Major Daniel J. Rehm, pilot of Spooky 41, observed:

Anti-aircraft fire

"When we arrived, the buildings in the compound were all afire and the men were grouped in a blockhouse below the burning operations centre. We set up a quick orbit of the area and began firing on targets about 200 to 300 metres from the camp. Almost immediately we began receiving intense anti-aircraft fire from four different points. I began with a long burst at a target from my Miniguns but when the tracers started to fly close to us I moved to another altitude and began to

peck with short bursts at the enemy locations."

The enemy held to the attack in the teeth of an onslaught of gunships, tactical fighters, B-52s, and assorted Army aircraft. For the next several nights, at least one Spooky supplied flare illumination and firepower over Duc Lap. In 228 flying hours the gunships expended 761,044 rounds and 1,162 flares.

Chugging along at 180 knots, its insides gutted of all but the essential equipment to turn it into a fighter plane, the Fairchild AC-119 was a heavy old ship that wasn't really suited to the demanding gunship task. Too many people got involved in its development, and it was delivered later than expected – but Stinger and Shadow crews got the job done.

EYE WITNESS
by those who fought

Mayday over Laos

The night of 8 May 1970 witnessed an extraordinary display of airmanship when a Stinger from Udorn was heavily damaged by anti-aircraft fire.

Captain Alan D. Milacek and his nine-man crew had been reconnoitring a heavily defended road section near Ban Ban, Laos, when they discovered, attacked and destroyed two trucks. Captains James A. Russell and Ronald C. Jones, the sensor operators, located three more trucks. As the aircraft banked into attack orbit, six enemy positions opened up with a barrage of AA fire. The co-pilot, Captain Brent C. O'Brien, cleared the fighter escort for attack and the gunship circled as the F-4s worked to suppress the AA fire.

Another truck killed

Amid the heavy enemy fire, Captain Milacek resumed the attack and killed another truck. At 0100, just about two hours into the mission, "the whole cargo compartment lit up" as enemy rounds tore into the Stinger's right wing. A "sickening right dive of the aircraft" ensued and Milacek called "Mayday, Mayday, we're going in." He shouted orders to SSgt Adolfo Lopez, Jr, the IO [illuminator operator], to jettison the flare launcher.

Ready to jump for it

Captain Milacek directed the entire crew to get ready for instant bailout. As the gunship dropped about 1,000 ft within a few seconds, Captains Milacek and O'Brien pooled their strength to pull the aircraft out of its dive.

By using full-left rudder, full-left aileron, and maximum power on the two right engines, they regained stabilised flight.

The full-engine power fuelled two/three foot flames – torchlights for enemy gunners as the crippled Stinger desperately headed for friendly territory. Navigator Captain Roger E. Clancy gave the correct heading but warned they were too low to clear a range of mountains towering between them and safety.

Fuel running out

What's more, the crew discovered that fuel consumption would likely mean dry tanks before reaching base.

The crew tossed out every possible item to lighten the load and the aircraft slowly climbed to 10,000 ft. TSgt Albert A. Nash, the flight engineer, reported the fuel-consumption rate had fallen.

No-flap landing at 150 knots

Captain Milacek elected to land the damaged plane and when he approached the base area he ran a careful check of controls. He found that almost full-left rudder and aileron would allow him to keep control. With uncertain flap damage, Milacek chose a no-flap landing approach at 150 knots (normally 117 knots). Utilising every bit of pilot skill he landed the plane. Upon leaving the Stinger, the crew saw about one-third of the right wing had been torn off.

Below: Devastation like this, caused by the VC against a friendly village in South Vietnam, could be prevented if gunships were in the area and in contact with friendly troops.

EYE WITNESS
by those who fought

Spectre Target

"Ubon ground crews readied aircraft 1629 for the evening's flight. They put aboard Mk 24 and Mk 6 flares and 6,000 rounds of ammunition. The aircraft lifted off just before dusk. Within 10 minutes they were 'crossing the fence' (the Mekong River separating Thailand from Laos), and made contact with the airborne battlefield control and command centre (ABCCC), which assigned *Spectre 01* an operating area.

"They reported 'on station' at 1720, and loitered, making contact with the F-4 Phantoms which would be suppressing AA fire. At 1815 they started to patrol a 15-mile segment of Route 922. Just 25 minutes later they identified Target 1 – four vehicles, moving east. Going into his left orbit at 4,500 feet, the pilot sighted in on his target. In four minutes he fired off 1,000 rounds of 20-mm.

"Target 2 came up at five minutes to seven. A single truck. Two minutes of orbiting attack and another 1,000 rounds of cannon fire finished him off.

"Just down the road, *Spectre 01* discovered three stationary trucks and what seemed to be an organised park. He illuminated the area with flares, and soon came under 37-mm anti-aircraft fire. For more than 20 minutes the aircraft made short 'pecking' attacks, firing off another 1,000 rounds in the process. An explosion and fire told of the AA gun emplacement's destruction.

Attack completed

"Two more stationary trucks became Target 4, at a few minutes after eight o'clock, and then two of the F-4s – Schlitz and Combine their call signs – worked with *Spectre 01* to destroy two more AA sites. At 2020, the gunship returned to Target 3 – the truck park – and gave it another 1,000 rounds, just in case anything had survived the first attack.

"*Spectre 01* left the target area at 2035, having spent three-and-a-quarter hours there, and re-crossed the Mekong and touched down at Ubon at 2115, all her stores expended."

Below: A good loiter time was one of the outstanding advantages of using a big aircraft like the C-130 in the gunship role. In addition to carrying electronics and its crew, it could also give a huge amount of space to the storage of ammunition for the gun armament.

The NVA had some of the best AAA crews in the world. Throughout the war, flak caused the vast majority of US air casualties, and units like this, the 1st Battalion of the Singh Gianh AA brigade, did their share.

DETECT AND DESTROY

1 Reconnaissance

The problem with locating targets on the Ho Chi Minh Trail was that the targets did not want to be spotted. Movement was by night, and much of the Trail was covered in heavy vegetation. The solution was technology. Aircraft were fitted with the most advanced sensors available at the time. The sensor package usually involved Forward Looking Infra-Red, Low Light TV, and a laser designator, making the detection of formerly invisible movements possible. 'Black Spot' was an experimental conversion of the C-123 Provider cargo aircraft, used operationally out of Ubon Air Base in Thailand. As the anti-air threat along the trail increased, 'Tropic Moon' conversions of the faster Martin B-57 bomber became more suitable.

TRUCKS - MU GIA PASS AREA
9 FEBRUARY 1967

130 TRUCKS

ROUTE 15

MU GIA PASS

LAOS

Above: Phantoms dropped sensors, disguised as vegetation, along the Trail to detect enemy vehicles and troops on the move.

Recon, relay, response

Stopping an enemy convoy on the Ho Chi Minh Trail involved a closely co-ordinated effort involving numerous aircraft and ground control stations.

1 B-57s fitted with infra-red sensors monitor known Trail routes and 'seed' surrounding areas with ultra-sensitive dart-like sensors that stick in soft earth and become almost invisible. They transmit the presence of vehicles or people.

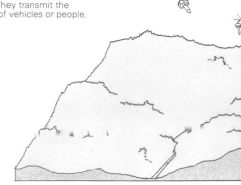

Killing trucks on the Trail was no problem for the USAF – if it could find them. A big effort went into the task.

The trucks roar through the darkness beneath the jungle canopy. They are filled with military supplies, destined for the communist forces in South Vietnam. There is no sign of American air activity, and there hasn't been for days. Travelling by night, always keeping under cover, the convoy should escape detection. Yes, the commander thinks, this is one convoy that will get through.

The sound of the engine of his truck drowns out the faint drone coming down from high above. Even if he hears the plane, he will assume that it is too high to do any damage. And with the darkness and the leafy canopy, how can the Americans know that the trucks are here?

What the North Vietnamese commander does not know is that he has already been given away. It is the rumble of his own trucks which has done so. Even though there are no Americans within miles of the trail, the passage of the convoy has been heard. Two miles in the sky, hard American eyes are looking into a screen. The electronics fitted into the AC-130 Spectre gunship light the scene as bright as day. Zeroing in on the lead truck, the commander gives the order to fire. 40-mm shells make short work of the Soviet-supplied Zil truck, and even as exploding fuel lights the scene the North Vietnamese commander finds time to ask himself, "How did they know where to find us?"

Dark and deadly, the Martin B-57 was involved in a number of sophisticated surveillance-gathering programmes, including 'Patricia Lynn' and 'Tropic Moon', as well as being one of the first USAF aircraft to drop bombs on South Vietnam. Pilots and navs rated the Americanised Canberra highly.

3 Relay

Once the Igloo White sensors had been activated by passing traffic along the Trail, they would begin transmitting. Initially they would send their data to large EC-121R aircraft (conversions of the civil Lockheed Constellation airliner), but as the anti-air threat grew these were pulled back out of harm's way. However, the radio transmitters on the sensors were not very strong, so some kind of airborne relay was essential. A cheap, unmanned drone was developed from the Beech U-22 single-engined monoplane, and these QU-22Bs became the initial stage of the relay.

Left: The Beech U-22 was a modified civil Bonanza lightplane ordered by the USAF for the Pave Eagle signal relay mission. Most of the cabin was fitted with equipment to allow the relay of signals from the Igloo White seismic sensor programme. They could be piloted or flown remotely.

2 Target Location

Aircraft cannot be in the air all the time, and in Vietnam they could not provide continuous cover of the hundreds of miles of the Trail. Project Igloo White was the code name for all of the electronic warfare operations carried out along the Trail to make up this deficiency. Automatic acoustic and seismic sensors were dropped along the main Trail routes. Acoustic sensors would remain inert until triggered by the sound of passing vehicle engines; seismic sensors would be triggered by the vibration of passing lorries or armoured vehicles.

2 Heavy enemy ground defences meant that faster, better-armed attack bombers like the Phantom took over the sensor-seeding task from more vulnerable aircraft, with the bonus that they could also knock out targets of opportunity.

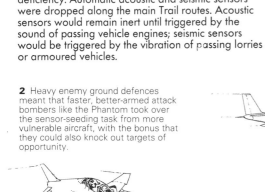

3 & 4 Two vital elements in the search and destroy mission was the EC-121 Constellation and the Beech U-22, the Beech acting as a go-between and beaming its revelations to the Connie.

5 The EC-121's info was processed by an Igloo White station and target information went out to an AC-130 gunship. The aircraft then used its own sensors to find, fix and kill the target. Similar target ID would go out to other tactical aircraft.

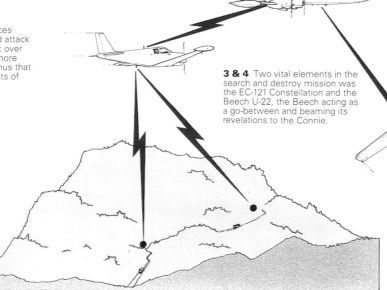

below. But they don't. Like other aircraft types among today's new generation of highly manoeuvrable fighters, the F/A-18 can stop on a sixpence.

The missiles shoot past in front of the Hornets and waste themselves in the distance. Closing in at maximum speed, the MiG-23s attack now with their cannon. The air is filled with the 'corruption' from flying cannon shells as the Hornet flight leader shouts, "Break left! Haul around them!"

"Roger, breaking."

"Let's haul around behind the bastards and get 'em with the 'Winder."

Quick manoeuvre

The Hornets flip onto their sides, wings vertical now, seemingly at an angle so dizzy that the fighters will fall out of the sky. They don't. Although the MiGs are flying much faster, the Middle East pilots are unprepared for the sudden change. It may take a MiG-23 only half a mile to perform a successful turn, but the Hornets have made a complete turn-about in just a few hundred feet. Now the MiGs are caught in their gunsights.

"Fox Two!" the flight leader calls, using the term for firing a Sidewinder heat-seeking missile. Each F/A-18 Hornet fires a Sidewinder.

With this new AIM-9R model, there is no need to hang about, so the Hornets flip around again and are flying away from the scene when a pair of explosions marks the end for a pair of MiGs. "Splash two," barks the flight leader into his radio. Because his jet fighter is amazingly manoeuvrable, to a degree that would have been unimaginable even a decade ago, he has achieved a quick and decisive victory.

Until recently, fighters were designed with

Above: France's Mirage 2000, in service since the mid-1980s, is a multi-role fighter optimised for high-altitude, high-speed operations, but its fly-by-wire controls also give it excellent all-round manoeuvrability. Solidly built, the Mirage can pull over 13 g in a turn without coming apart.

the emphasis on power and speed. Today, the be-all and end-all of fighter combat is manoeuvrability. It's a revolution.

As recently as the early 1980s, a jet fighter like the F-4 Phantom or the MiG-23 shrieked through the sky like a flying blowtorch, took on an enemy using missiles and guns, and used up a mile or more to pull through a turn during a dogfight. The pilot knew that each missile shoot or gun-firing pass might be his only chance: if he missed, it might take him half a minute and several miles to get back into the fight.

All that has changed. Today's fighters – the F-15, F-16, F/A-18 Hornet, the MiG-29, and Su-27 – have been through the revolution and can now slug it out at close range, making tight turns and other abrupt manoeuvres never previously possible.

Tomorrow's fighters, among them the EFA (European Fighter Aircraft), and the American F-22 and F-23, will be even more

FLASHBACK

The Supermarine Spitfire was a superfighter, not so much for its performance – although it was a superb dogfighter – but because it caught the imagination of a nation.

The Spitfire in World War II

Outnumbered in the Battle of Britain by the Hurricane, the Spitfire nevertheless became the yardstick by which all World War II fighters were measured. Blessed with the sweetest handling ever bestowed on a fighter, the Spitfire could outfly and outfight any opponent, and proved itself in all climates. The airframe proved a natural for growth, and a succession of ever more powerful developments kept the type at the top of the tree throughout the conflict, the last variants being much more than twice as heavy as the prototype. In contrast, its classic opponent became more and more of a brute, as power and weapons were crammed into the slender airframe of the Me 109.

SUPERFIGHTERS Reference File

287

MiG-29 'Fulcrum'

FORMER USSR

Operational since 1985, the **MiG-29 'Fulcrum'** is comparable in size to the F-18 Hornet and closely resembles the larger Su-27. Currently operated primarily as a single-seat counter-air fighter, the MiG-29 has full dual-role air combat/ground attack capability and was designed with considerable growth potential.

The **'Fulcrum-A'** is a land-based single-seater which comes in three models. The initial production aircraft featured twin ventral tailfins similar to those on the Su-27; this was followed by production aircraft with the ventral fins deleted and dorsal fins extended forward into aerodynamic wing fences. A third sub-variant has extended-chord rudders. The **MiG-29UB 'Fulcrum-B'**

is the combat trainer two-seater, the second seat being positioned forward of the normal cockpit, under a one-piece canopy. The **'Fulcrum-C'** resembles the 'Fulcrum-A', but has a deeper fuselage section aft of the canopy, to enclose an equipment bay. The **Maritime 'Fulcrum'** is also similar to the 'Fulcrum-A', but has upwards-folding outer wing panels for carrier stowage and no wing-fence flare dispensers. Anticipated deployment is aboard the carrier *Tbilisi* and later ships.

Specification
MiG-29 'Fulcrum'
Type: single- or two-seat counter-air/ground attack fighter
Powerplant: two Isotov RD-33

8300 kg (18,300 lb st) turbofans
Performance: maximum speed Mach 2.3; service ceiling 17069 m (56,000 ft); range 2092 km (1,300 miles)
Dimensions: span 11.36 m (37 ft 3¼ in); length 17.32 m (56 ft 10 in); height 4.73 m (15 ft 6¼ in)
Weights: empty 8176 kg (18,025 lb);

maximum loaded 18,000 kg (39,700 lb)
Armament: one 30-mm (1.16-in) gun in port wing LEX; six AA-10 or AA-11 AAMs on wing pylons; plus bombs, rockets and other stores
Users: 13 countries worldwide

The Swedes have always been innovative when it comes to fighter design, and the Saab Viggen foreshadowed many of the characteristics of modern superfighters when it first flew in 1967. Its powerful motor and high-lift wing gave it notable short take-off performance, and the canard wings on the forward fuselage add greatly to the Viggen's agility.

the pilot. His computer will overrule him, for example, if it sees a better way to complete a certain manoeuvre, or if the pilot attempts a manoeuvre which seems likely to put him into a stall or other dangerous situation.

Future fighters will use canard flight surfaces – small wings mounted near the nose – and thrust-vectoring nozzles to make them even more versatile.

Long-range radar power

Aside from these new breakthroughs in fighter manoeuvrability, the new generation of superfighters can also kill at a distance. Most (with the exception of all but a few F-16s) can begin an aerial duel from beyond visual range (up to 80 or 100 miles away) using radar-guided missiles. A pilot no longer needs to remain on a collision course while guiding his missile towards an enemy; he can fire it and forget it. If the enemy is below him, his new radar can weed out unwanted reflections

manoeuvrable. It is only a small exaggeration to say that future fighters will be able to turn within their own length or, for all practical purposes, fly backwards.

The damage that such skills can inflict on an enemy who lacks the same capability is almost overwhelming. The pilot of a superfighter, duelling with a fighter from an earlier generation, reigns supreme. Very simply, an older jet fighter simply can't touch one of today's high-manoeuvre superstars.

High manoeuvrability – the key to success in aerial combat in the 1990s – is largely the result of computer advances. But it's also true that today's fighters are constructed of materials that are stronger (allowing higher g, or gravity, forces) and lighter. Many use epoxy or carbon-fibre composites, replacing major parts of the aircraft previously cut from heavy metal. Lightweight materials, coupled with improved turbofan engines offering greater thrust, make a fighter very responsive to its

pilot's touch. Innovative changes in the size and shape of flight surfaces – the slats, ailerons and rudders that steer the plane through the air – are also part of the larger story of improvements in modern fighters.

As for the computer advances, modern fighters are now equipped with air data computer centres, digital data networks, and computerised fly-by-wire controls that make the aircraft react instantly to the pilot's touch. With old-style controls, the pilot's 'pull' on his stick did not result in movement of an aileron until translated into action manually or hydraulically, by pulleys, wires and cables inside the aircraft. The microchips of today's fly-by-wire controls transmit the pilot's command to an aileron or other flight surface, using electrons. The effect is instantaneous, eliminating the 'gap' between decision and action.

Furthermore, the decision as to what a modern aircraft will do next is not left solely to

The Professional's View:

The F-16

"The F-16 is not a hard airplane to fly. It's the information overload that mostly causes the problems. If you have maybe 15 years' experience in flying fighter aircraft, you've developed techniques and habits that work. Part of that, at least, comes from familiarity with the aircraft; when you have a target in a particular place on the scope, you know what to do with it to shoot the guy.

"In the F-16, you know how to fly an intercept. You can solve that problem in three-dimensional geometry without having to think too hard. But then suddenly you're hit with so much information about the target, you don't know where to look. But in the end you realise just how much easier the F-16 makes the job."

Captain Mark Harting, 177th Fighter Interceptor Group, New Jersey, 1989

288

USA 🇺🇸

General Dynamics F-16 Fighting Falcon

One of the world's top fighters, the **F-16** first entered service in January 1979. The initial single-seat **A** and two-seat **B** models were followed by improved **F-16C** and **D** (single- and two-seaters respectively), and in 1986 there emerged the **F-16 ADF** (Air Defense Fighter). This, a further upgrade of the F-16A was intended to replace ageing F-4s and F-106s in 11 continental-USA-based Air National Guard squadrons. A parallel upgrade was made with the F-16B. Up to 270 such modifications were originally ordered, and deliveries to date exceed 2,500 aircraft.

The F-16 ADF has its APG-66 radar enhanced with a data link for the AMRAAM, provision for the AIM-7

Sparrow AAM, improved electronic counter-countermeasures and better survivability against cruise missiles. An HF radio, an IFF interrogator and a crash-survivable flight data recorder are among the new equipment items added.

Among the further developments is the **F-16 MLU** (mid-life upgrade) fighter, intended for European air forces already using the earlier models, and similar in scope to the F-16 ADF; a version unofficially known as the **A-16** is intended for the battlefield/close air support role.

Specification
General Dynamics F-16C
Type: single-seat air superiority fighter

Powerplant: one 12520 kg (27,600 lb st) General Electric F110-GE-100 or one 10637 kg (23,450 lb st) Pratt & Whitney F100-PW-200 augmented turbofan
Performance: maximum speed Mach 2 plus; ceiling 15240 m (50,000 ft) plus; range 925 km (575 miles)
Dimensions: span 10 m (32 ft 9¾ in); length 15.04 m (49 ft 4 in); height 5.09 m (16 ft 8½ in)
Weights: empty 8317 kg (18,335 lb); loaded 19187 kg (42,300 lb)
Armament: one M61A 120-mm gun; AIM-9 AAMs; seven external pylons
Users: 17 countries worldwide

The F-16: a modern multi-mission fighter

■ 2 × AIM-9L Sidewinder close-range AAMs on wingtip launcher rails
1 × internal 20-mm M61 cannon with 515 rounds

■ 2 × AIM-9L Sidewinder close-range AAMs on wingtip launcher rails
1 × internal 20-mm M61 cannon with 515 rounds
2 × AIM-7 Sparrow or AIM-120A AMRAAM medium-range AAMs underwing
■ 1 × 1136-litre (300-US gal) fuel tank on centreline
2 × Sargent-Fletcher 1400-litre (370-US gal) drop tanks on inboard underwing stations

■ 2 × Mk 83 1,000-lb (907-kg) bombs on mid-wing pylons (nuclear weapons can also be carried)
2 × AIM-9L Sidewinder close-range AAMs on wingtip launcher rails
1 × internal 20-mm M61 cannon with 515 rounds

■ 4 × Mk 82 Snakeye 500-lb (227-kg) retarded bombs on twin-carriers on mid-wing pylons
2 × AIM-9L Sidewinder close-range AAMs on wingtip launcher rails
1 × internal 20-mm M61 cannon with 515 rounds
■ 2 × Sargent-Fletcher 1400-litre (370-US gal) drop tanks on inboard underwing stations

■ 2 × AGM-78 Standard anti-radar missiles on mid-wing pylons
2 × AIM-9L Sidewinder close-range AAMs on wingtip launcher rails
1 × internal 20-mm M61 cannon with 515 rounds

■ 2 × Paveway laser-guided bombs on mid-wing pylons
2 × AIM-9L Sidewinder close-range AAMs on wingtip launcher rails
1 × internal 20-mm M61 cannon with 515 rounds
■

Dogfighter

The majority of USAF F-16s carry only a very small warload with two Sidewinders on the wingtip launchers which do not restrict the aircraft's phenomenal ability to withstand prolonged 9 g manoeuvres. Whether or not the missiles can be launched throughout the entire flight envelope has not been revealed, but the AAMs are backed up by an internal gun for use in a high energy close-in environment.

Long-range interception

USAF F-16s can frequently be seen carrying only their wingtip Sidewinders, but they do back these up with other weapons, even in the air-to-air role. The AIM-7 is the most common such 'extra', although it is being replaced by the newer AMRAAM.

Strike

The F-16 is quite a potent attack machine, able to carry a sizeable weapon load. The penalties are such that to retain manoeuvrability, attack-configured F-16s generally carry far fewer stores than they are capable of lifting. The B-43 nuclear weapon is the 'nuke' most likely to be carried.

Ground attack

F-16s seldom operate in the attack role during peace, but they can do so, and have turned in some impressive results during bombing and air-to-ground gunnery competitions. The retarded Snakeye is a particularly effective weapon.

Wild Weasel

The F-16 could perform as a dedicated Wild Weasel aircraft with Standard ARMs, Shrikes or HARMs, and the USAF has been considering the acquisition of such a variant. The standard F-16 might well carry one or two defence-suppression missiles in addition to a normal attack payload.

Precision attack

Paveways could be replaced by Hobo guided bombs, or by TV- or laser-guided AGM-65 Maverick missiles, but without a dedicated air-to-ground radar and nav/attack system there are limits to what can be achieved.

289

FRANCE

Dassault-Breguet Mirage 2000

The **Mirage 2000** features a variable-camber delta wing to help boost its top speed to Mach 2.35. The prototype first flew in March 1978 and the first production aircraft in mid-1982, the year the first export orders were placed – by Egypt and India. Built first and foremost for high intercept speeds – it can reach Mach 2 at 49,000 feet four minutes after the brakes are released – the Mirage 2000 is not in the same class as the F-16, in terms of manoeuvrability. However, the tail-less delta configuration makes it the master of the high-altitude, high-speed mission.

Incorporating such modern systems as fly-by-wire controls, the aircraft has a formidable close-combat capability. In an emergency situation, the pilot can

pull up to 13.5 g without tearing the aircraft apart. Acceleration is excellent, and the aircraft rolls very rapidly at high speed, carrying two cannon and two AAMs for the basic air intercept mission.

As with most modern combat aircraft, the Mirage 2000 comes in alternative versions to the single-seater. These include the **2000C1** conventional ground attack aircraft, the **2000B** two-seat trainer, the **2000N**, which has low-level strike capability carrying nuclear weapons, and the **2000R** reconnaissance model.

Specification
Dassault-Breguet Mirage 2000
Type: interceptor/air superiority fighter

Powerplant: one 9700 kg (21,400 lb st) SNECMA M53 turbojet
Performance: maximum speed Mach 2.35; ceiling 18300 m (60,000 ft)
Dimensions: length 14.17 m (46 ft 6 in); span 9 m (29 ft 6 in)
Weights: empty 7636 kg (16,835 lb); loaded 11760 kg (25,928 lb)

Armament: two 30-mm DEFA 554 cannon with 125 rpg; two Matra Super 530D and two Matra R.550 Magic AAMs
Users: Egypt, France, Greece, India, Peru and United Arab Emirates

---

290

UNITED KINGDOM/ GERMANY/ITALY/SPAIN

Eurofighter

Intended as an 'across the board' replacement for most of the current interceptors used by NATO countries, the **Eurofighter** is now being developed under Britain's **Experimental Aircraft Programme (EAP)**. Flying at the British Aerospace airfield at Warton for the first time on 8 August 1986, the EAP is enthusiastically described by test pilots as a 'heavy metal pilot's aircraft'. It is currently well into the development flying programme, the single aircraft being called a technology demonstrator. This 'one-off' aircraft is not a prototype, but it will gather a vast amount of data on handling and performance which will be continually fed into the computers which 'design'

the service aircraft.

The distinctive single fin (an earlier twin-finned design having been dropped), all-moving canard foreplanes and a large box-like ventral air intake are among the features of the EAP which will be carried over into production Eurofighters for the RAF, Luftwaffe, and Italian and Spanish air forces. Two production prototypes, P.01 and P.02, will be followed by eight more prototypes, the first scheduled to make its maiden flight late in 1991.

As a true prototype of the 1990s, the Eurofighter is expected to remain in widespread service for the first decades of the 21st century, when all other current fighters in its class will be very long in the tooth.

Specification
Eurofighter
Type: single-seat air defence interceptor
Powerplant: two Turbo-Union 7484 kg (16,500 lb st) RB199 Mk 104D turbofans
Performance: Mach 2 plus

Dimensions: length 17.52 m (57 ft 6 in); span 11.18 m (36 ft 8 in)
Weights: empty 10000 kg (22,050 lb); loaded 15422 kg (34,000 lb)
Armament: ASRAAMs and Skyflash AAMs
User: under development

from the ground and locate the enemy with uncanny precision.

The principal air combat weapon is still the heat-seeking missile, typified by the AIM-9 Sidewinder, which can be used at medium range (five to 20 miles). New versions of these heat-seekers are 'all aspect', meaning that they no longer need to home in on an enemy's hot exhaust. They can now strike from any direction.

Cannon armament

In this new world of high manoeuvrability, it is essential that a fighter is armed with a gun for close-quarter combat. The aerial machine-gun is as extinct as the dinosaur, replaced now by cannon firing an explosive shell. Among the best-known of these is the American M61, officially called the Vulcan but better known as the 'Gatling', after the first rapid-fire weapon developed during the American Civil War. .

Manoeuvring remains the keystone of air combat. In the past decade, Russian fighters have 'come out of the closet', appearing publicly in air shows at Farnborough and elsewhere in Europe and North America. The

The F-15S/MTD was fitted with fly by-wire controls, canard wings and vectoring engine nozzles to provide outstanding agility.

The Northrop/McDonnell Douglas YF-23 was the other ATF competitor. A very large fighter, it made extensive use of stealth technology.

291

SWEDEN

Saab JAS 39 Gripen

This single-seat multi-role fighter for counter-air, attack and reconnaissance missions is the latest in a long line of Saab designs that have served the Swedish armed forces for decades. It is the lightest of the current generation of canard delta fighters by quite a margin, and features full state-of-the-art avionics, including multi-function CRT cockpit displays. Following some delays, the **Gripen** (Griffon) prototype flew for the first time on 9 December 1989.

Intended as a replacement for all versions of the Saab Viggen and Draken now in service, the Gripen will fulfil all combat roles to ensure that each aircraft ordered is used to the full. Instead of producing different versions,

each Gripen will be adapted to take AAMs, ground attack weaponry and recon equipment to undertake the variety of missions, as the need arises. The first production aircraft was delivered to the Swedish air force in 1992, after the successful conclusion of the flight test programme which involved a total of five prototypes.

To build the Gripen, the JAS industry group was formed. It comprises Saab's Aircraft Division and Volvo Flygmotor, which will supply the engine, plus radar and electronics specialist concerns. The announced programme for the Gripen is for construction of an initial series of 30, followed by 110 examples to be delivered by the year 2000.

Specification
Saab JAS 39 Gripen
Type: single-seat air superiority, attack and reconnaissance fighter
Powerplant: one Volvo Flygmotor turbofan
Performance: Mach 2 plus
Dimensions: length 13.72 m (45 ft);
span 8 m (26 ft 3 in)
Weights: empty 6350 kg (14,000 lb); loaded 8165 kg (18,000 lb)
Armament: one 27-mm (1.08-in) Mauser BK27 cannon; up to four AAMs and other munitions, as dictated by mission requirements
User: Sweden

292

FRANCE

Dassault-Breguet Rafale

Another in the worldwide family of multi-role, canard-configuration combat aircraft for the latter 1990s and early 21st century, the **Rafale** is expected to replace Jaguars and Mirage IIIs and Vs in French air force service beginning in 1995. Under an intensive programme, the manufacturers concentrated on producing a fighter that could leave any of its rivals standing when it came to close-range air combat. The **Rafale A** has a better thrust-loading than most other fighters have when using afterburning, and it has demonstrated that it can sustain very tight turns at low altitude – where other, less capable types would stall out.

Dassault has followed some of the trends set by the F-16 in providing the

Rafale with a reclining pilot position, a teardrop canopy giving 360-degree vision (though it is not frameless), and a side-stick controller rather than a conventional control stick.

A basic requirement for Rafale was that it would be able to scramble from a 500-metre landing strip with guns loaded and carrying two AAMs, in a war scenario in which conventional airfields were under enemy attack.

Production models, designated **Rafale B**, are smaller and lighter than the A model which was designed as a technology demonstrator. Low weight means better performance and cheaper operating costs, giving good export potential.

Specification
Dassault-Breguet Rafale A
Type: single-seat multi-role fighter
Powerplant: two 7258 kg (16,000 lb st) F404 turbofans
Performance: Mach 2 plus
Dimensions: length 15.8 m (51 ft 10 in); span 11 m (36 ft 1 in); height
4.98 m (16 ft 4 in)
Weights: empty 9095 kg (20,050 lb); loaded 14000 kg (30,870 lb)
Armament: one 30-mm (1.16-in) DEFA 554 cannon; four MICA or two R.550 Magic AAMs
User: under development

The electronics revolution has changed the modern fighter cockpit out of all recognition. Now, instead of a myriad of dials, the pilot has three or four computerised video displays, which can give him all the information that the dials did, only much more simply.

result has been a very public display of aerial manoeuvrability. The new Soviet fighters have really turned heads with their 'Cobra' manoeuvre, so-named because the fighter sticks its nose straight up, like a snake striking, while continuing along in level flight.

A MiG-29 performed a spectacular 'Cobra' manoeuvre at the Canadian National Capital Air Show in Ottawa in the summer of 1989. The operation begins with a low-level pass in which the nose is rotated rapidly to 90 degrees vertical and beyond, followed by a rapid return to level flight. If the pilot were in combat, he would be able to swing his guns through a 90-degree arc to score an unexpected aerial kill. American experts say that the F-15, F-16 and F-18 could perform the 'Cobra' manoeuvre, if safety constraints on the software for their computer air data centres were to be relaxed.

We can only imagine the future capabilities of superfighters still on the horizon. These fast jets are nothing less than spectacular testimony to how rapidly our technology has advanced.

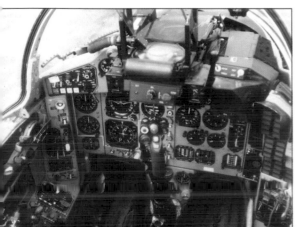

A fancy cockpit is not absolutely necessary in a superfighter. This example, from the amazing MiG-29, looks positively archaic, but the aircraft still flies like a dream

Development

It is a long way from the fragile fabric-and-string machines that contested the skies over the Western Front of World War I to the latest hi-tech miracles taking to the air in the 1990s, but in many ways all these fighters are similar. Speed, agility and hitting power are as important to the EAP as they were to the Sopwith Camel.

1943 Focke-Wulf Fw 190 D-9

The original Focke-Wulf Fw 190 entered combat in 1941 and proved a formidable fighter. The later D-9 was fitted with a long Jumo 213 engine, which improved its performance dramatically.

1949 NA F-86 Sabre

The North American Sabre was one of the first swept-wing fighters, and flew much faster and higher than late-war jets like the Gloster Meteor and the Lockheed P-80 Shooting Star.

1957 MiG-21

The MiG-21 is one of the great post-war fighters. Some 15,000 have been built, more than any other military aircraft since the war, and it remains in service with over 50 air forces.

1986 BAe EAP

The British Aerospace Experimental Aircraft Programme is being used to test concepts and equipment for the European Fighter Aircraft, which will equip a number of air arms through the first decade of the 21st century.

of the fighter

1917 Sopwith Camel

Left: The Sopwith Camel was slower than its contemporaries, but its manoeuvrability helped it shoot down more German planes than any other Allied scout.

Above: The long-nose 'Dora Nine' retained all of the Focke-Wulf Fw 190's fighting power but increased its speed from 400 to 450 miles per hour.

Below: The North American F-86 Sabre was capable of nearly 700 miles per hour. Armed with six .50-calibre machine-guns, it held its own in the skies over Korea against the cannon-armed MiG-15.

Left: Light and manoeuvrable, the MiG-21 was one of the earliest Mach 2 fighters. Although it has limited range, the MiG-21 has seen extensive combat, especially in the Middle East.

Above: Developed by British Aerospace, the EAP is a state-of-the-art combat aircraft. It has highly computerised fly-by-wire controls, and is very manoeuvrable. This prototype is armed with BAe Sky Flash missiles.

111

The MiG-29 is a superfighter in spite of its old-fashioned control systems, because its advanced aerodynamic qualities give it an agility unmatched by any fighter currently in service.

THE CUTTING
EDGE

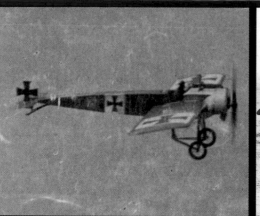

Fighters of World War I were extremely agile. The British Camel (above, far left) and the French Spad (left, with American balloon-destroying ace Frank Luke) of 1917 and 1918 were a considerable advance on the Fokker 'Eindekker' (above left), which had wrought such havoc only a year earlier. Later Fokker designs presented more of a challenge, and included the fragile but highly manoeuvrable Triplane (above right, seen being flown by Manfred von Richthofen) and the Fokker D.VII (above), which was probably the best fighter of the war.

World War I

Aeroplanes had been flying in Europe for less than a decade when World War I broke out in 1914. The first aircraft were flimsy, wide-winged creations, with little or no fighting power. The only combat was between observers, taking pot-shots at each other with pistols and rifles. Later aircraft had machine-guns, and some were designed as pushers, with the propeller behind the pilot. This meant that guns could be pointed directly forward for the first time.

It was the appearance of the Fokker 'Eindekker' monoplane which changed matters. Armed with a single fast-firing machine-gun, it was also equipped with the first practical interrupter gear, allowing the gun to be fired through the arc of the propeller without hitting the blades. Now pilots could be hunters, engaging in aerial duels in which the aircraft became the weapon, or more often creeping up on the enemy to take him from behind. The Fokker almost cleared the sky of Allied aircraft, until it was outclassed by new D.H. and Nieuport designs. From then on, the war was a series of leapfrogs, with successive German scouts like the Albatros, the Fokker Triplane and the superb Fokker D.VII being countered by Allied aircraft such as the Spad, the Camel and the S.E.5.

Fighters have always pushed the limits of available technology. Their speed, agility and firepower have improved amazingly in less than a single lifetime.

There have been rare occasions in history when warfare has been changed out of all recognition by the development and use of new weapons. Few would have thought, as England and France embarked on the Hundred Years War, that the armoured knight would have been laid low by English yeomen wielding a peasant weapon. But the great battles at Crecy, Poitiers and Agincourt were decided by the longbow.

Then again, nobody could have foreseen that the all-conquering bow would in turn be ousted from its dominant position by firearms. Guns, then making their first appearance, were large, inaccurate and slow to fire. Yet within a century, the musket had come to dominate the battlefield.

The industrial revolution of the 18th and 19th centuries changed warfare, as it did every other

aspect of life. Now, instead of an idea revolutionising combat every century or so, each conflict became a forcing-house in which designs for new weapons appeared with greater and greater frequency.

In just 30 years, infantry weapons went from the muzzle-loading musket, with which both armies were equipped at the start of the American Civil War, to the machine-guns used by European powers in their colonial wars of the 1890s. Artillery improved as dramatically over a similar period. At sea, fighting ships changed from broadside sailing vessels, which Nelson would have found familiar, to grey-painted steel monsters with huge guns in turrets, foreshadowing the great battleships of World War I and World War II.

Similar developments have taken place in the 20th century. The most revolutionary of these did not even

exist in 1900, but has since become a decisive factor in battle. From the first flight at Kitty Hawk in 1903 to the latest stealth fighters, the military capabilities of the aeroplane have advanced beyond belief.

Evolution of the fighter

From the start, the most visible examples of advances in aerial technology have been provided by the fighter. The development of machine-guns that could fire through the propeller turned the frail scouts of the early years of World War I into the fighting machines of 1917 and 1918.

The high-performance fighters of World War II made use of much more powerful engines, but even as the Spitfires, Hurricanes and Messerschmitts fought it out in the Battle of Britain they were about to be made obsolescent by the development of the jet.

Fighters continued to develop in a spectacular fashion after 1945. The MiGs and Sabres which contested the skies over Korea were made to look pedestrian by the supersonic machines that were soon to enter service, and these in turn were outmatched by the Mach 2 generation of the 1960s.

Absolute top speed has not increased greatly since then, but in every other field, from weapons to manoeuvrability, the fighter has become immensely more capable. As the world advances towards the year 2000, a whole new generation of computer-controlled machines is either under development or entering service. With such exciting types as the European EFA and the American ATF taking to the air, it is clear that superfighters will remain at the cutting edge of aircraft technology.

Above: The Ta 152, developed from the Focke-Wulf Fw 190, represented the peak of German piston-engined fighter development, having heavier armament and being able to fly much faster, higher and farther than fighters of less than three years before.

Above: The Hawker Sea Fury was perhaps the ultimate piston-engined fighter. Capable of nearly 500 miles per hour, it had nevertheless been made obsolete by the development of jets like the Messerschmitt Me 262 (inset).

Below: Although jets appeared at the end of World War II, it was classic prop-driven fighters like the North American P-51 Mustang, which appeared in swarms in 1944 and 1945, that were to decide the course of the air war.

World War II

The years before the outbreak of World War II saw rapid advances in fighter design. The Spitfires, Hurricanes and Messerschmitts that fought the Battle of Britain were a great deal more capable than the biplanes of the 1930s, yet they themselves were to be surpassed by a similar margin before the end of the war. Magnificent machines like the P-51 Mustang, the Hawker Tempest and the Focke-Wulf Ta 152 took piston-engine technology almost to its limit. But there was a limit, and something radical would have to be done to increase fighter performance.

In fact, the way ahead had been signposted before the start of the war. In August 1939, a small aircraft lifted off the ground at Marienehe airfield near Rostock. The Heinkel He 178 was the first jet in history, and while it was hardly a practical aircraft, it was a harbinger of things to come. By 1944, both Germany and Britain had operational jet fighters, with the Americans not far behind. Although the British Meteor saw no combat other than shooting down flying bombs, the Messerschmitt Me 262 proved in the heat of battle that the jet was vastly superior to the piston-engined fighter. Germany also developed an operational rocket interceptor that was faster than anything ever seen before, but which had limited endurance and was dangerous to fly.

Top: The Gloster Meteor beat the Me 262 to squadron service by a few days. It was not as good as the German design, but still outperformed the piston-powered fighters of the day.

Above: The first operational American fighter was the Lockheed P-80 Shooting Star, which reached squadrons in Italy just before the end of World War II and went on to fight in Korea.

The jet age

Development of the jet proceeded rapidly after World War II. The Americans and the Soviets, who had lagged behind the British and the Germans, applied their vast resources to the problem, but war broke out in Korea before any breakthrough was apparent. In the early days, the World War II-vintage Lockheed F-80 Shooting Star proved more than a match for the piston-engined Lavochkins and Yaks on the North Korean side, as well as for the early MiG and Yak jets of the same generation. The introduction of the MiG-15 changed all that. Powered by a derivative of a British engine, the MiG flew higher and faster than anything else in Korea. In order to stop it clearing the skies, the Americans had to field their own superfighter, the F-86 Sabre. Both of these swept-wing machines outperformed the first generation of jets, and they took air combat into a new dimension.

Although the USA, the Soviet Union and the United Kingdom generally dominated jet fighter development, nations like France and Sweden made it clear that they were not going to simply sit back and be customers; instead they developed their own machines, which compared very well with the products of the 'big three'.

Above: The Swedish aircraft industry has produced some fine designs. The Saab 32 Lansen was an excellent machine, first flown in 1952 and comparable with the Hawker Hunter, MiG-17 or later North American Sabres. Like the Hunter, it could exceed the speed of sound while in a dive.

Right: Almost as soon as the second generation of jets took to the skies, they were outclassed by the new supersonic fighters. The Dassault Mirage III first flew in 1956, and in 1958 it became the first European fighter to exceed twice the speed of sound, beating the English Electric Lightning by a month.

SABRE FIGHT

Far left: A MiG-15 erupts into flame as bullets from the six .50-calibre guns in the nose of an F-86 Sabre chew through the Soviet-built fighter's wing root. These two types, superfighters of their day, engaged in dogfights over Korea at speeds and heights never before attempted in combat. The MiG had slightly superior performance at altitude, but the training of the Sabre's pilots more than made up any difference.

Left: The years after World War II saw an evolutionary leap in aircraft design, fuelled by the unleashed power of the jet engine. Aircraft like the North American F-86 Sabre fighter and the North American B-45 Tornado bomber, both flying in the late 1940s, were a considerable advance on the machines which equipped air forces at the end of World War II, only four years previously.

Below: Sabres on the ramp of pierced-steel planking at Suwon are prepared for a fighter-bomber mission. The F-86's speed and agility made it suited to ground attack as well as air superiority roles, with three of the five Sabre formations in Korea at the end of the war being designated FBW, or fighter-bomber wings.

The air war over Korea was notable for the first jet-versus-jet combats in history, and for two classic fighters which were to clash in the skies of the Far East.

"The MiGs will be up. We feel it. They're planning to ambush the fighter-bombers up ahead of us.

"It's a frigid winter day and we're perched along the edge of the stratosphere, flying parallel to the Yalu River, looking over into China.

"Now, we see the glint of sun against steel as the MiGs pull off the runway and climb. They think they're in perfect position to catch the fighter-bombers in a trap – but so far, they don't know *we're* up here."

The speaker is an F-86 Sabre pilot, 4th Fighter Interceptor Wing, 1951.

"Those MiGs have been beating the pants off us. The ongoing campaign between the F-86 and MiG-15 has cost *them* something, too. But what I think about is an empty bunk next to mine. Today it's payback time . . ."

The prolonged contest between the F-86 Sabre and the MiG-15

during the Korean War (1950-3) was one of the epic campaigns in the history of warfare.

Fighter battle

On one side: Chinese pilots. Their MiG-15 hit the world like a storm when China entered the war in November 1950. Most in the West had not known of the Soviet-built fighter; it drew headlines proclaiming it vastly superior to anything else in the air. The Chinese took off from airfields along the Yalu River and were in combat within minutes, often with the advantage of higher altitude. Though inexperienced, the Chinese were well-trained and helped by Russian pilots, some of whom flew beside them in combat. The Chinese also enjoyed sanctuary when at home, thanks to politicians who ruled that their airbases were on the wrong side of the border and couldn't be bombed.

On the other side: American pilots. Their North American F-86

Left: This MiG-15 was flown to Kimpo airfield by a defecting North Korean officer in September 1953, after the war had ground to a halt. Given US Air Force markings, and tested extensively, it proved to be in some ways better than the Sabre. However, it was not that much better, and superior American pilot training told in the end.

Right: A Sabre pumps shells into a MiG-15's wing in April 1953. American aircrew claimed 792 MiGs during the two and a half years of war, the majority shot down by F-86 pilots. During the same period, 78 Sabres were downed.

Sabre was a better fighter than anyone yet knew, but it had not fully matured at the beginning of the campaign and was rarely described in the fearsome language reserved for the MiG. Far more experienced than their opponents, many of them aces from World War II, the Americans faced a serious handicap: forced to travel long distances to reach the fight, they were already battling exhaustion and running low on fuel when they reached 'MiG Alley', just south of the Yalu. They could only place themselves in position – bait, some called it – and wait for the enemy to strike.

To add to their other disadvantages, the Americans were hopelessly outnumbered. By mid-1951, the Chinese had MiG-15s at three principal airbases along the Yalu (newspaper readers learned the unfamiliar names of Antung, Fen Cheng and Tatangkou), as many as 400 aircraft in all, confronting a Sabre force of about 70 aircraft, of which no more than 24 were combat-ready on any single day. By 1952, the Sabre force had grown to 160.

American bombers had enjoyed freedom to roam at will over North Korea. Now the MiG-15 swept the skies of prop-driven B-26 Invaders and B-29 Superfortresses as if they were not free to fly at all. Because of the MiG, it became suicide to journey near the Yalu. But allowing the enemy free reign would be even worse. Something had to be done.

The task of the Sabre force, consisting of the 4th and 51st Fighter Interceptor Wings, was to keep the MiGs away from friendly bombers. The Sabres swept the Yalu at high altitude and provoked dogfights with the MiGs to keep them occupied. Much like knights in a joust, the Sabre pilots let themselves be seen, staked out a position, and waited for the other guy to strike. As late as mid-1951,

Right: As with all aerial combat claims, the ten-to-one kill ratio between Sabres and MiGs was probably exaggerated. Nevertheless, American pilot superiority is still evident in the more likely proportion of four or five to one. There is no doubt in the sequence shown here, however, since the communist pilot is clearly seen baling out. The MiG was shot down in May 1953 by the F-86 flown by 2Lt Edwin E. Aldrin, Junior – who 16 years later was to go on to fame as the Lunar Module pilot on Apollo 11 and the second man on the moon.

after more than six months of combat, the F-86 wings were still ironing out tactics.

"Our flight leader calls a warning as the MiGs come across the Yalu. The first thing we realise is, it didn't work. They knew we were here all along. We're at 36,000 feet, but they're close to 40,000 now, and they're *not* going after our fighter-bombers. They're coming for us.

"'Okay,' my flight leader's voice booms. 'They're coming in. Three, four, break right! Two, get over here and follow me up. Let's go get 'em!'

Sabre versus MiG

"Converging at well over a thousand miles an hour, Sabres and MiGs pass through each other. My earphones boom with warnings as our other two guys return to the fight. As we turn to re-engage, my leader is flinging his jet around. We've got the slats out – the unique leading-edge slats which allow the F-86F to grab a piece of the sky and pull itself almost to a halt in the middle of a high-speed manoeuvre. 'Holy shit!' I say to myself.

"It's surprise time. Using our new-found manoeuvring capability, my flight leader and I have practically jerked ourselves to a halt in the middle of the sky. The MiGs were pulling out and thought they were going to turn

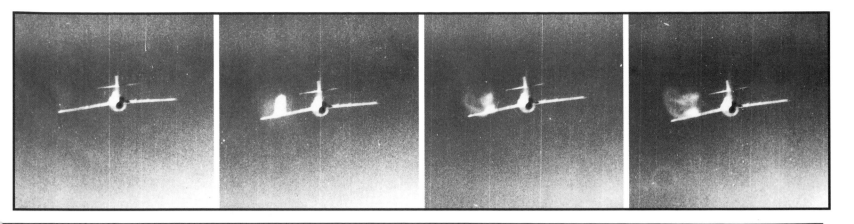

inside us, but the surprise works. Now the MiGs are pulling out *right in front of us. . .*

"'We got 'em. We're on top of the bastards!'

"A series of quick bursts from my flight leader saws the wing off one of the MiGs and sends the plane spinning end over end, out of control and spraying debris in

all directions. The MiG pilots are confused. Our two remaining F-86F Sabres come in above and across everybody else, spraying metal casings as their guns hammer out bursts. I get off a couple of shots at a MiG. Off to my right, one of our other guys has got a solid kill – another MiG, engulfed in flames, in a slow and

fatal glide towards the Yalu.

"The MiGs are scattering, going home. And we're low on fuel – a perpetual problem for Sabre pilots. 'Pull it in, guys,' orders the flight leader, and we, too, turn for home. . ."

The duel went on from November 1950 until the end of the war in July 1953. The MiG-15 was never able to live up to its potential. When a MiG-15 blew a Sabre out of the sky, the pilot was usually a Russian – sent not only to train the Chinese but also to gain combat experience. The Soviets withdrew once it appeared likely that an armistice would be signed, and in the last full month of the war – June 1953 – Sabres shot down 77 MiG-15s with no losses.

The final air-to-air score was 792 MiGs and 108 Allied fighters (including 78 Sabres) downed in combat. This 10-to-1 kill ratio by successful F-86 pilots has been questioned in recent years, but even if a revisionist view of history were to cut the figure in half, it would still be a towering achievement.

The Chinese side has never told the outside world of its air aces or its combat successes. On the US side, the contest between the F-86 Sabre and the MiG-15 produced 40 air aces, one of whom totted up 16 aerial combat victories.

Left: MiGs in a revetment are revealed by an American reconnaissance camera. Those on North Korean bases could be attacked; unfortunately, many of the MiGs were based beyond the Yalu, on Chinese territory.

Below: This F-86F of the 336th Fighter Interceptor Squadron, 4th Fighter Interceptor Wing, was flown by Captain D.R. Hall out of Kimpo airbase. The yellow bands are identification marks, carried by all Sabres in Korea.

THE ENERGY GAME

Air combat is all about energy. If you've got it, you can manoeuvre, and get the better of your foe. If you haven't, you are easy prey and he's likely to defeat you.

In spite of the reputation fighter pilots have of being latter-day cavaliers of the clouds, air combat is a sneaky business. It is more like coming up behind someone in a dark alley and bashing him over the head with a club than meeting face-to-face like knights in a jousting tournament. Eighty per cent of successes in air combat come from surprising the opponent. It does not matter whether he is in a Sopwith Camel on the Western Front in 1918 or a McDonnell Douglas F-15 Eagle over Saudi Arabia; if a pilot can catch his opponent by surprise, he has won the battle. Most victims are not even aware of being stalked, and inexperienced pilots have a very short life expectancy in combat.

The emphasis of a fighter pilot's training is on the ability to surprise an enemy without being surprised in turn. Positioning his aircraft to make an attack from the enemy's sunward side has been a primary aim of every fighter pilot since the earliest days. Not for nothing were Royal Flying Corps pilots on the Western Front in World War I warned to "beware of the Hun in the sun". Speed, electronic silence and modern electronic countermeasures all add to the ability to surprise the enemy, and small size is a great advantage. One problem with fighters like the American F-15 Eagle is that they are big machines, easy to spot at long distance. However, they have to be big to have the other qualities of power, performance and manoeuvrability which make them such superlative fighting machines.

These qualities come to the fore on the occasions when surprise is not possible. To

A McDonnell Douglas F/A-18 Hornet powers into the sky with its afterburners blazing. The Hornet is one of the most manoeuvrable of current Western fighters.

be an effective dogfighter, a combat aircraft must have good speed and acceleration, outstanding manoeuvrability, and the ability to outshoot an opponent.

Air combat is a matter of energy. The faster a fighter is moving, the more sharply it can manoeuvre, and the quicker it can get into a firing position or out of danger. In general, if a fighter loses energy, it is in trouble. Slow, and struggling to make a turn, it will be a sitting duck for an opponent who can still manoeuvre.

It looks very like the Hornet, but the MiG-29 'Fulcrum' is even more agile than the American machine. It is probably the most manoeuvrable fighter in the world today.

Two Tornado F.Mk3 fighters climb to make an interception. Tornados are not designed as dogfighters, their main task being to make long-range interceptions and to take out targets from beyond visual range. As a result, range and weapons performance are more important than agility, although in good hands, a Tornado is no slouch in close combat.

1 Manoeuvrability

From the earliest days of air-to-air combat, manoeuvrability has been the prime requirement for survival in a dogfight. Until comparatively recently, an aircraft had to get on an opponent's tail to be reasonably sure of making a kill. Air-to-air missiles were most effective in a cone extending back from an opponent's tail, and the aircraft which could turn sharply and accelerate rapidly had the best chance of getting into that position.

The latest superfighters take the idea of manoeuvrability a considerable step forwards. Much of the most recent research into fighter aerodynamics has been in the area of 'High Alpha' manoeuvres, maximising lift at high angles of attack. This is now an air show favourite, with fighters making a slow pass down the runway with their noses hoisted high in the air, yet still flying. But this is much more than a display trick: it means that the wing is still generating lift at that angle, and if you translate the manoeuvre from the vertical plane to the horizontal, it means that the fighter can do some *very* sharp turns.

The 'Cobra'

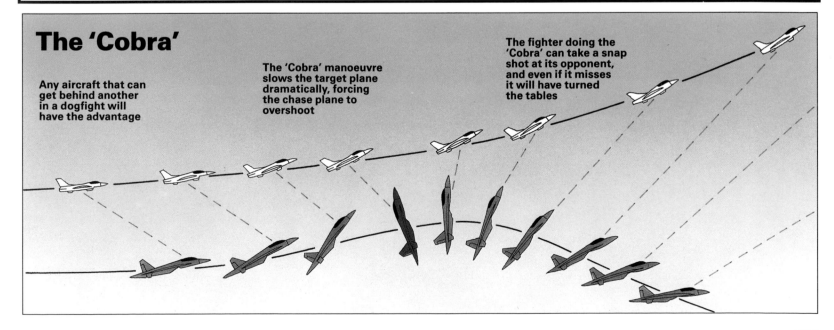

Any aircraft that can get behind another in a dogfight will have the advantage

The 'Cobra' manoeuvre slows the target plane dramatically, forcing the chase plane to overshoot

The fighter doing the 'Cobra' can take a snap shot at its opponent, and even if it misses it will have turned the tables

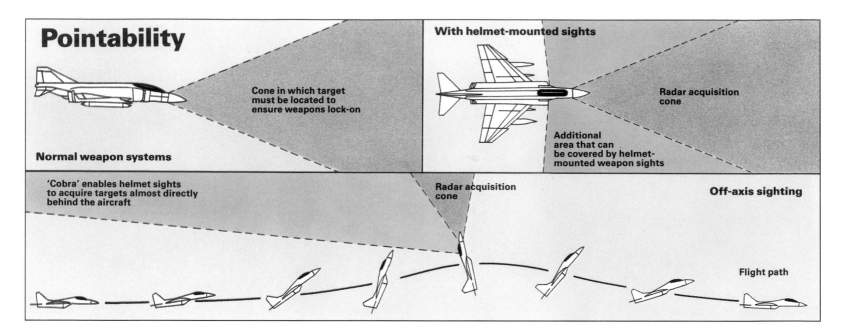

Pointability

Normal weapon systems

Cone in which target must be located to ensure weapons lock-on

With helmet-mounted sights

Radar acquisition cone

Additional area that can be covered by helmet-mounted weapon sights

'Cobra' enables helmet sights to acquire targets almost directly behind the aircraft

Radar acquisition cone

Off-axis sighting

Flight path

All the conventional fighter wisdom is about to change, however. The new generation of combat aircraft takes dogfighting into a whole new realm. Powerful, fast-reacting engines provide stunning acceleration. With computerised fly-by-wire controls, an aeroplane can perform the most fantastic manoeuvres and still remain in the sky. Stunts that would have been thought impossible less than a decade ago have since thrilled enthusiasts at air shows around the world. But those crowd-pleasers have serious applications, and the dogfight of the future might be very different from those of the last 70 years.

2 Pointability

The development of 'all-aspect' weapons, which need not be fired from behind the target, has freed the fighter pilot from having to manoeuvre behind an enemy. He will still seek to do so, since surprise attacks are just as much the name of the game today as they were in the past. Until comparatively recently, however, the pilot still had to fly directly towards the enemy so that his radar or the seeker heads on his missiles could lock onto the target. Thus infra-red or radar-guided missiles could be fired only at targets in an acquisition cone of a few degrees on either side of the direction of flight.

The manoeuvrability of modern fighters enables them to direct their weapons well away from the line of flight. Instantaneous turn capability, pointing the nose well away from the axis of flight and then snapping back, can extend the acquisition cone dramatically. Fighters like the MiG-29 can reliably pull 50 degrees away from the flight axis, and have been known to pitch more than 80 degrees before resuming normal flight, while the 'Cobra' manoeuvre performed by the Sukhoi Su-27 involves a movement through more than 100 degrees!

Even more dramatic improvements result when helmet-mounted sights are added to the equation. These are linked to the plane's weapons systems, pointing guns and missiles to wherever the pilot turns his head. With the good visibility afforded by modern cockpits, only if an enemy aircraft is directly behind a fighter is it reasonably safe from attack. And if a fighter can perform a 'Cobra' manoeuvre, it can even shoot at somebody there!

3 Unpredictability

Stability is a good thing in a training aircraft, but it can kill a fighter pilot. A trainer should be easy to fly, and have slow, predictable reaction to control movements in order to allow inexperienced pilots to recover from mistakes. In contrast, from the earliest days of air combat, a fighter has had to be able to do the unpredictable. The Sopwith Camel was slow, unstable and extremely difficult to fly, but it was also the most successful fighter of World War I, largely because its opponents never knew what it was going to do next. The best fighters of World War II were less eccentric, relying more on high performance and conventional agility.

Modern superfighters combine the unpredictability of the Camel with high performance and superb manoeuvrability. They are designed to be unstable, and a pilot can control them only with the aid of computers, since stable flight is not natural to them. As a result, they are much quicker in the turn and roll than more conventionally controlled machines. In a dogfight they might snap up, or down, or invert, or yaw. The only factor that limits their manoeuvrability is the pilot, since he will black out long before the plane is taken to its limit.

Below: The amazing agility of modern fighters enables them to fire their weapons from all attitudes. Here, a General Dynamics F-16 fires an AIM-9 Sidewinder missile while in the middle of a high-g turn.

Right: Swing-wings, such as those of the Grumman F-14 Tomcat, give a fighter greater low-speed agility, but they are also an unmistakeable signal to an opponent that you are not travelling very fast.

ATTACK AIRCRAFT

No other warplane deliberately enters the lethal zone of the enemy. But if you're going to fly ground attack, you have to meet him literally head-on.

Flying at almost five hundred knots – approaching 'tunnel vision' speed – and a bare 30 ft off the water of Falkland Sound, well below the skyline, the pair of Harrier GR.Mk 3s streaked towards the settlement at Goose Green, rising and falling with the small changes of their control surfaces.

Suddenly they were overhead, and then gone, all in the same instant. All that was left, as the young Paras on the ground strained to see, was a flash impression of grey and green, of stubby, swept wings festooned with weapons and the deafening thump and roar of the jets echoing in their heads.

With all the advantages of speed and sur-

prise on his side, the Harrier pilot had bad luck to fear more than anything else. As he crossed the buildings of what had been Goose Green settlement, he nudged the aircraft up, clawing the extra height that would develop the cluster bomb pattern. He reached the Argentine position before the anti-aircraft gun crews had time to react, and the lads from D Company, 2 Battalion The Parachute Regiment, watched as canisters fell from the wings and burst open before impact, each

Wreathed in gun gas 'smoke', an A-10 makes a shallow diving attack: a laser-guided Paveway bomb awaits release from the wing pylon.

The first aggressive act of World War II was an attack by Stukas 11 minutes before the Germans crossed the Polish border.

scattering 147 BL755 cluster bomblets. As they hit the ground they exploded, wiping out the gun in an instant.

Now it was the second Harrier's turn. He followed the same general line as the first, crossing the coast from the north-west and popping up as he crossed the buildings – they were such a convenient marker – and released his cluster bomb units a little to the right of where the first had done such damage.

It's possible that the men on the ground weren't even aware of the presence of the third Harrier as it came in at a wide angle to the others' tracks and fired 36 two-inch SNEB rockets to cross the 'T' of the others' weapons.

World War I origins

Just as suddenly as they came, the three grey-green aircraft were gone, into the south-east, down the Sound, over the hills and far away. To the Argentines at Goose Green, it was the last straw and they sought surrender.

Ground attack aircraft were used as long ago as 1916, to strafe troops in the trenches of the Somme and Flanders, and by the time of World War II the techniques had been considerably improved and refined. As Hitler swept into Poland his troops were preceded by an onslaught of Stuka dive-bombers san-

Above: In World War II, few fighter bombers could equal the P-47 Thunderbolt, seen here turning a French bomber into scrap metal on the dispersal point of a German airfield.

Right: One of Vietnam's star performers in the ground attack role was the old Douglas Skyraider. This four-seat 'E' model has just released napalm over a target.

FLASHBACK

Blitzkrieg!

When the Germans attacked Poland in September 1939 to spark off World War II, their surprise attack coined a new word – Blitzkrieg. This 'lightning war', spearheaded by Junkers Ju-87 Stuka dive-bombers, paved the way for armour and infantry to go in against shattered and demoralised defences. In the early years of the war, the Luftwaffe and the German army combined to quickly wipe out the armed forces of most of Western Europe, and Blitzkrieg tactics took the Germans to the gates of Moscow before the tide turned in the Allies' favour. The Stuka spearhead was quickly lost when fighter opposition was strong.

Bombs fly off a dive-bombing Ju 87 'Stuka' on their way to hapless Poles below.

ATTACK AIRCRAFT Reference File

35
USA

General Dynamics F-16 Fighting Falcon

This was designed as an air-combat fighter of unparalleled agility, but since its service debut in 1978 has matured as an exceptional versatile warplane that includes ground-attack amongst its many capabilities. Here the six-barrel cannon in the port leading-edge root extension has its part to play, but much more significant is the heavy load of disposable ordnance that can be carried on the hardpoints (one under the fuselage and six under the wings) for free-fall or guided delivery under control of the F-16's advanced sensors (inbuilt and podded) and fire-control system.

All F-16s are combat capable, and variants include the original **F-16A** and **F-16B** single- and two-seaters, supplemented from 1984 by the **F-16C**

and **F-16D** single-and two-seaters with greater power, a larger tailplane and considerably more versatile combat electronics including the LANTIRN (Low-Altitude Navigation and Targeting Infra-Red for Night) podded system for the accurate delivery of the latest weapons.

The US Air Force is considering a dedicated attack version of the Fighting Falcon under the provisional designation **A-16**, which will have a host of specialist features for this important task.

Specification
General Dynamics F-16C
Type: single-seat multi-role warplane
Powerplant: one 12519-kg (27,600-lb)

thrust General Electric F110-100 or 10637-kg (23,450-lb) thrust Pratt & Whitney F100-220
Performance: maximum speed 2125+ km/h (1,320+ mph); range 3887+ km (2,415+ miles)
Dimensions: span 9.45 m (31 ft 0 in); length 15.03 m (49 ft 4 in);
Weights: empty 8316 kg (18,335 lb);

maximum take-off 19187 kg (42,300 lb)
Armament: one 20-mm cannon and up to 9276 kg (20,450 lb) of disposable stores
Users: Belgium, Denmark, Egypt, Greece, Indonesia, Israel, Netherlands, Norway, Pakistan, Singapore, South Korea, Thailand, Turkey, USA and Venezuela

itising the ground ahead. Messerschmitt Bf 109 fighters ranged freely over the fleeing Poles, shooting up their positions with cannon and machine-guns from low level. And so it went on until Hitler's advance was halted in Russia.

Then the tables were turned. As the Germans became bogged down, the Soviet air force unleashed the greatest ground-attack aircraft of all time. Enormous formations of up to 500 Ilyushin Il-2 'Stormoviks' orbited over friendly territory in 'cab ranks' until called into action. Packs would then detach, bypass the enemy's front line, fan out and strafe the enemy rear with cannon, bombs and rockets. They became known as the 'Black Death' to the frightened Germans.

The Stormoviks were built like tractors. Extremely tough and rough, they were hammered out in makeshift factories and workshops all over Russia. Stalin continually wanted more: "The Red Army needs the Il-2 as it needs air or bread. I demand more. This is my last warning." He got them at the rate of

---

36
British Aerospace Harrier

UNITED KINGDOM

The Harrier was the world's first operational warplane with STOVL capability, and thus able to operate away from vulnerable airfields from the comparative safety of small clearings offering the possibility of a short take-off run so that the maximum warload can be carried. The type entered service in 1969 as the Harrier GR.Mk 1 with an armament of two 30-mm cannon in the underfuselage strakes and free-fall ordnance on five hardpoints (one under the fuselage and four under the wings).

The variant currently in service is the **Harrier GR.Mk 3** with a more powerful model of the Pegasus vectored-thrust turbofan, improved defensive electronics and a revised nose accommodating a laser ranger and marked-target seeker for much improved weapon-delivery accuracy with laser-guided as well as free-fall weapons. The type can also carry a BAe reconnaissance pod with forward oblique and low-level fan cameras as well as an IR linescanner.

The current conversion trainer is the **Harrier T.Mk 4**, which lacks the single-seater's radar-warning receiver but otherwise possesses full combat capability.

Specification
British Aerospace Harrier GR.Mk 3
Type: single-seat STOVL close support and reconnaissance warplane
Powerplant: one 9752-kg (21,500-lb) thrust Rolls-Royce Pegasus Mk 103 turbofan
Performance: maximum speed 1186+ km/h (737+ mph); range 1333 km (828 miles)
Dimensions: span 7.70 m (25 ft 3 in); length 14.27 m (46 ft 10 in)
Weights: empty 6139 kg (13,535 lb); maximum take-off 11793 kg (26,000 lb)
Armament: two 30-mm cannon and provision for 3269 kg (8,000 lb) of disposable stores
User: UK

A load of 750-lb low-drag bombs tumbles from the racks of an F-4 Phantom, premier attack aircraft of the Vietnam war. This is the long-nosed 'E' model with internal M61 gun.

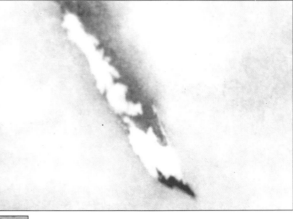

Above: Not all Vietnam strikes were successful and many US aircraft were lost, like this one, to the 'wall-to-wall' AAA fire that surrounded most targets.

2,300 per month, and more than 36,000 by the end of the war.

But the greatest ground-attack pilot of them all was a German. Hans-Ulrich Rudel became the most decorated German of the war, gaining all four additions to the Knight's Cross of the Iron Cross. Flying Stukas and Focke-Wulf Fw l90s over the Russian front,

---

37

FRANCE/UK

SEPECAT Jaguar

First flown in 1968, the Jaguar was planned in two forms as a supersonic trainer and ground-attack aeroplane, the latter with two lower-fuselage cannon and five hardpoints (one under the fuselage and four under the wings, the latter given good clearance for the carriage of bulky loads by the wing's high-set position). The UK's **Jaguar GR.Mk 1** is now used mainly for reconnaissance, while the French air force's **Jaguar A** is used in its designed role on the power of two 3315-kg (7,305-lb) thrust Adour Mk 102 turbofans and comparatively simple electronics including, in some aircraft, the ATLIS II designator pod for laser-guided weapons.

The export version, first flown in

1976, is the **Jaguar International** with greater power (initially the 3900-kg/8,598-lb thrust Adour Mk 804), two overwing hardpoints for air-to-air missiles, and more capable electronics including a head-up display, digital inertial navigation and weapon-aiming system, projected map display, laser ranger and marked-target seeker, and optional features such as a radar-warning receiver. An increasing number of Indian aircraft have search radar, the advanced DARIN nav/attack system, and provision for anti-ship missiles.

Specification
SEPECAT Jaguar International
Type: single-seat multi-role tactical warplane

Powerplant: two 4205-kg (9,270-lb) thrust Rolls-Royce/Turboméca Adour Mk 811 turbofans
Performance: maximum speed 1699 km/h (1,056 mph); range 2816 km (1,750 miles)
Dimensions: span 8.69 m (28 ft 6.1 in); length 16.83 m (55 ft 2.6 in)

Weights: empty 7000 kg (15,432 lb); maximum take-off 15700 kg (34,613 lb)
Armament: two 30-mm cannon and up to 4763 kg (10,500 lb) of disposable stores
Users: France, UK and (Jaguar International) Ecuador, India, Nigeria and Oman.

38

FRANCE/WEST GERMANY

Dassault-Breguet/Dornier Alpha Jet

The Alpha Jet first flew in 1973 as a dual-role type to meet a French trainer requirement and a West German attack aeroplane need. These two models are respectively the **Alpha Jet E** and the **Alpha Jet A**, which can carry disposable ordnance on four underwing hardpoints as well as an underfuselage pod for a 27- or 30-mm cannon in West German and French aircraft respectively. The West German model had more advanced electronics than the French version, including a head-up display and provision for ECM pods.

The Alpha Jet A entered service in 1979 and is now known as the **Alpha Jet Close Support Version**, which is being upgraded with more powerful engines and the ability to carry modern

weapons including self-defence AAMs. The export version was the **Alpha Jet MS-2**, and such aircraft in Egyptian service are being upgraded to **Alpha Jet 2** standard with greater power and a number of improved electronic features. Yet to be ordered into production is the **Lancier**, a French-developed attack and anti-ship model with radar and other sensors as well as the capability to carry an anti-ship missile or advanced free-fall weapons of the laser-guided type.

Specification
Alpha Jet A
Type: two-seat light attack and reconnaissance warplane
Powerplant: two 1350-kg (2,976-lb)

SNECMA/Turboméca Larzac O4-C6 turbofans
Performance: maximum speed 927 km/h (576 mph); range 2940 km (1,827 miles)
Dimensions: span 9.11 m (29 ft 10.75 in); length 13.23 m (43 ft 5 in)
Weights: empty 3515 kg (7,740 lb);

maximum take-off 8000 kg (17,637 lb)
Armament: one 27-mm cannon and up to 2500 kg (5,511 lb) of disposable stores
Users: (all Alpha Jet models) Belgium, Cameroun, Egypt, France, Ivory Coast, Morocco, Nigeria, Qatar, Togo and West Germany

he accounted for hundreds of enemy tanks and even sank a Soviet battleship with a single bomb.

Ground-attack aircraft were also vital to success in the West. Before and after the D-Day landings in Normandy, squadrons of USAAF Thunderbolts and RAF Typhoons scoured the countryside of northern France, hunting for targets of opportunity such as ammunition trains, fuel and supply dumps and concentrations of troops and vehicles, and, when they could, acting in close support of the troops on the ground. It seemed good sport, produced spectacular gun-camera film, and became the essence of the ground attack spirit. So it continued through the Korean War and into Vietnam.

Faster than sound

Naturally, aircraft design had come on during the 20 years between the end of World War II and the start of the Vietnam War. Propellers had given way to jets, and straight wings had become swept. Fighters could now fly faster than sound, and many could nearly do 1,500 miles an hour. They could even drop nuclear bombs on cities. But could they drop a 250-lb bomb on a truck in the jungle without

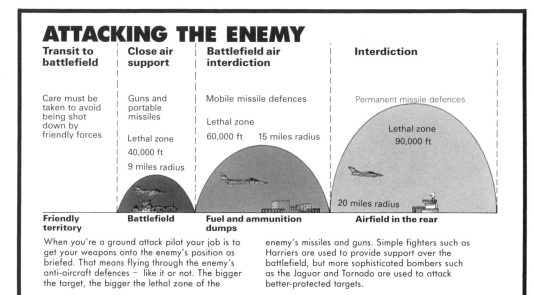

ATTACKING THE ENEMY

Transit to battlefield	Close air support	Battlefield air interdiction	Interdiction
Care must be taken to avoid being shot down by friendly forces	Guns and portable missiles	Mobile missile defences	Permanent missile defences
	Lethal zone 40,000 ft 9 miles radius	Lethal zone 60,000 ft 15 miles radius	Lethal zone 90,000 ft 20 miles radius
Friendly territory	Battlefield	Fuel and ammunition dumps	Airfield in the rear

When you're a ground attack pilot your job is to get your weapons onto the enemy's position as briefed. That means flying through the enemy's anti-aircraft defences – like it or not. The bigger the target, the bigger the lethal zone of the enemy's missiles and guns. Simple fighters such as Harriers are used to provide support over the battlefield, but more sophisticated bombers such as the Jaguar and Tornado are used to attack better-protected targets.

getting shot down? The Americans found that it was harder than it looked, and lost hundreds of aircraft and pilots proving it.

High-performance aircraft were just too fast and unmanoeuvrable to place ordnance accurately in a counter-insurgency situation.

And their long, predictable run-ins made them vulnerable even to a guerrilla with an automatic rifle, let alone a mobile 23-mm anti-aircraft gun. The F-100 Super Sabres and F-4 Phantoms were just shot out of the sky.

In a reaction that turned the clock back

39

FORMER USSR

Mikoyan-Gurevich MiG-23 and MiG-27 'Flogger'

The MiG-23 was conceived as a tactical fighter and began to enter service in 1970 as an air-combat fighter with a 23-mm twin-barrel cannon in the lower fuselage and about 3000 kg (6,614 lb) of disposable stores carried on four hardpoints (two under the fuselage and two under the gloves of the variable-geometry wings). Fighter-bomber models have two additional bomb attachments under the rear fuselage.

Before production ended in the late 1980s the type had been developed in several variants. Fighter-bomber versions of the basic MiG-23 are the **MiG-23B 'Flogger-F'** and **MiG-23BN 'Flogger-H'** derived from

the MiG-23M 'Flogger-B' fighter with a revised and shallower 'duck' nose lacking the fighter's search radar and infra-red sensor, but offering superior fields of vision to the pilot in a cockpit with improved armour protection and greater glazing.

The **MiG-27 'Flogger-D'** dedicated attack type takes the process a step further with an engine/inlet/nozzle arrangement optimised for lower performance, larger-diameter tyres of the low-pressure type, two additional hardpoints, and a six-barrel cannon. The aerodynamically refined **MiG-27M 'Flogger-J'** adds a laser ranger and marked-target seeker in the nose.

Specification
Mikoyan-Gurevich MiG-27M 'Flogger-J'
Type: single-seat ground-attack warplane
Powerplant: one 11500-kg (25,353-lb) thrust Tumanskii R-29B-300 turbojet
Performance: maximum speed 1880 km/h (1,168 mph); range 2500 km (1,533 miles)
Dimensions: span 13.965 m (45 ft 9.8 in) spread and 7.779 m (25 ft 6.25 in)

swept; length 17.10 m (56 ft 1 2 in)
Weights: empty 9980 kg (22,002 lb); maximum take-off 20700 kg (45,635 lb)
Armament: one 23-mm cannon and up to 4000 kg (8,818 lb) of disposable stores
Users: (MiG-23) Algeria, Angola, Bulgaria, Cuba, Czechoslovakia, East Germany, Egypt, Ethiopia, Hungary, India, Iraq, Libya, North Korea, Poland, Romania, South Yemen, Syria, USSR and Vietnam; (MiG-27) India and USSR

40

FORMER USSR

Sukhoi Su-17/20/22 'Fitter'

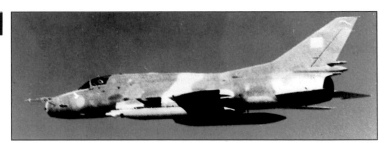

In 1966 the Sukhoi bureau flew the Su-7IG prototype of its Su-7 ground attack fighter modified with variable-geometry outer wing panels for better field performance and increased range in the cruise regime with the wings in the minimum-sweep position. Trials confirmed that this modification radically improved payload/range performance over that of the Su-7, and the type entered production as the **Su-17 'Fitter-C'** with the 10000-kg (22,046-lb) thrust AL-21F-1.

Later versions are the **Su-17M 'Fitter-C'** with the AL-21F-3 (exported as the **Su-20** with less capable electronics), the electronically improved **Su-27MK 'Fitter-D'** with a lengthened and drooped nose

(exported as the **Su-22 'Fitter-F'** with 11500-kg/25,353-lb thrust Tumanskii R-29BS-300 turbojet but electronics of reduced standard), **Su-17UM 'Fitter-E'** conversion trainer, the **Su-17UM 'Fitter-G'** improved combat-capable trainer based on the Su-17UM, the **Su-17BM 'Fitter-H'** based on the Su-17MK with the forward fuselage of the Su-17UM, more fuel and two additional hardpoints (exported as the **Su-22BKL 'Fitter-J'** with inferior electronics and the Tumanskii engine), and the **Su-17 'Fitter-K'** with improved electronics and ECM.

Specification
Sukhoi Su-17M 'Fitter-C'
Type: single-seat ground-attack

warplane
Powerplant: one 11200-kg (24,690-lb) thrust Lyul'ka AL-21F-3 turbojet
Performance: maximum speed 2220 km/h (1,379 mph); range 1370 km (851 miles)
Dimensions: span 13.80 m (45 ft 3 in) spread, 10.00 m (32 ft 10 in) swept; length 18.75 m (61 ft 6.25 in)
Weights: empty 10000 kg (22,046 lb);

maximum take-off 17700 kg (39,021 lb)
Armament: two 30-mm cannon and up to 4000 kg (8,818 lb) of disposable stores
Users: Afghanistan, Algeria, Angola, Czechoslovakia, East Germany, Egypt, Hungary, Iraq, Libya, North Yemen, Peru, Poland, South Yemen, USSR and Vietnam

The A-10 fires 1,200 rounds in 17 seconds.

Most attack aircraft pack unguided rockets in pods, the A-7 Corsair being no exception. This Air Force 'Sluff' (Short Little Ugly Fat F . . . er) is diving on a US firing range - which is a vital part of keeping US forces sharp for any emergency that might arise. One day, the rocket run might again be for real.

Combat Comparison

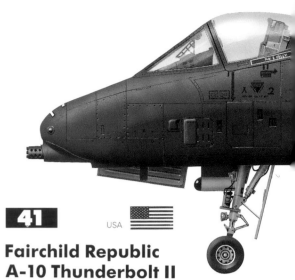

Fairchild Republic A-10 Thunderbolt II

The **A-10A Thunderbolt II** has been the US Air Force's most important ground-attack warplane since 1975, and is a firmly subsonic type designed round the seven-barrel cannon that occupies most of the forward fuselage and fires devastating anti-tank projectiles. The A-10A also possesses 11 hardpoints (three under the fuselage and eight under the wings) for the carriage of free-fall and guided weapons, including homing glide bombs and up to six AGM-65 Maverick air-to-surface missiles.

Despite its considerable size the A-10A is notably agile, and this is an important factor in the Thunderbolt II's ability to operate and survive at very low levels. Here the warplane is aided by its design, which features a titanium armour 'bath' for the pilot, great redundancy in its systems and structure to minimise

nearly 20 years, the Americans pulled the obsolete prop-driven piston-engined Skyraider out of retired storage and sent it to the front. Tough, survivable, agile and able to carry heavy loads of basically World War II vintage bombs, the Skyraider did valuable service. But it didn't solve the problem. Just being in that environment was too dangerous.

What was needed, it was thought by the generals, was a new, tough, armoured ground-attack aircraft packed with firepower that could launch 'smart' weapons from a distance, rather than dumb ones from within the 'threat envelope'. And so the A-10 Thunderbolt was born.

Slow but agile, the A-10 was built to survive. Relying on its ability to fly low, masking itself by trees and hilly ground, the A-10 uses stand-off Maverick air-to-ground missiles to avoid getting into trouble. But with doubled-up systems and the pilot sitting in an armoured 'bathtub', the aircraft could supposedly survive a beating from the Russian-built ZSU-23-4 anti-aircraft guns.

Too late to serve in Vietnam, it became the USAF's standard tank-killer in Europe. But by now the environment had become tougher still. The latest surface-to-air missiles and predicting anti-aircraft guns can now engage fighters flying at less than 200 feet, so simply flying low is no longer an answer. The number of man-portable missiles on the battlefield today is enormous. And then there are the lookdown/shootdown radar-equipped fighters, and the air-to-air capable helicopters. Any one of these can spoil a ground-attack pilot's day. It's just getting too hot.

So perhaps the ground attack fighter is a dying breed. Certainly the British Army is no longer looking forward to any fixed-wing close air support at all. However, the US Air Force is still totally committed to the close air support mission, as is the Russian air force, with its Afghan war-proven Su-25 'Frogfoot'. And then there was the Falklands war, and one plucky ground-attack aircraft that proved that there was some mileage left in the mission: the Harrier.

Building on traditional Russian ground attack concepts, the Sukhoi Su-25 is the first modern Soviet combat aircraft designed to survive over the modern battlefield and undertake a multitude of roles with equal success.

First-line USAF aircraft such as the F-16D saddle a heavy stores load, ready for any call by ground troops. Maverick, firing here, is a launch and leave air to ground missile guided by television signal. It is backed by wingtip-mounted Sidewinders.

Sukhoi Su-25 'Frogfoot'

Entering service in 1982 for evaluation in Afghanistan, the Su-25 is the USSR's equivalent of the A-10A but is a smaller warplane of higher performance with its engines in lateral ducts (inside stainless steel protective boxes) rather than above the fuselage. The fixed armament of this **Su-25 'Frogfoot-A'** model is a 23-mm twin-barrel cannon in the lower nose, replaced in the definitive **Su-25K 'Frogfoot-B'** of 1984 by a 30-mm twin-barrel weapon. The 10 hardpoints (five under each wing) can carry a sizeable load of free-fall and guided ordnance.

Like the A-10A, the Su-25 accommodates its pilot and most important offensive electronics in a titanium 'bath' inside an armour glass windscreen and canopy. The warplane is provided with sturdy landing gear for operations from rough fields, and under the wings can be carried four pods containing all the equipment

Designed specifically for the close air support role, the Fairchild Republic A-10 is a dedicated tank killer with extended battlefield loiter time. The design reflects a number of features that offer maximum survivability.

The 'fighter'-style canopy of the A-10 provides a better pilot view than that from the 'Frogfoot', particularly to the rear. The main built-in weapon of both the A-10 and Su-25 has a similar 30-mm calibre.

The engine mounting of each aircraft shows a different approach – the A-10 'hiding' its powerplants from groundfire by a high rear mounting, and the 'Frogfoot' relying on armoured nacelles.

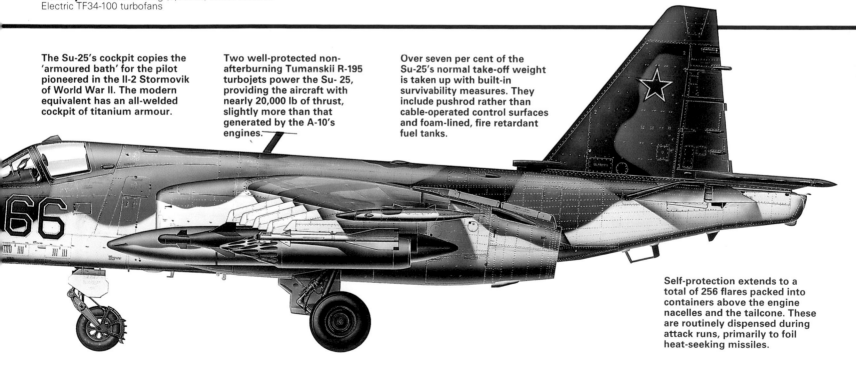

Apart from being larger, with nearly 10 ft more wingspan, the A-10 has a different 'sit' to the 'Frogfoot', being more or less level on the ground and so lacking the Russian machine's distinctive tilted back appearance.

Differences continue at the tail, where the A-10 has twin endplate fins and the Russian aircraft a single fin/rudder unit. The A-10's twin fins also help mask the engines from groundfire from the rear quarter.

the effects of battle damage, and an engine installation in which the spread of the two pod-mounted engines reduces the chances of both being lost and whose position shields the two turbofans from SAMs and anti-aircraft artillery fire.

Now worried about the type's subsonic performance, the USAF is planning a supersonic replacement for the A-10A in the near future.

Specification
Fairchild Republic A-10A Thunderbolt II
Type: single-seat close-support warplane
Powerplant: two 4112-kg (9,065-lb) thrust General Electric TF34-100 turbofans

Performance: maximum speed 681 km/h (423 mph); range 4091 km (2,542 miles)
Dimensions: span 17.52 m (57 ft 6 in); length 16.25 m (53 ft 4 in)
Weights: empty 9761 kg (21,519 lb); maximum take-off 22608 kg (50,000 lb)
Armament: one 30-mm cannon and up to 7258 kg (16,000 lb) of disposable stores
User: USA

The Su-25's cockpit copies the 'armoured bath' for the pilot pioneered in the Il-2 Stormovik of World War II. The modern equivalent has an all-welded cockpit of titanium armour.

Two well-protected non-afterburning Tumanskii R-195 turbojets power the Su-25, providing the aircraft with nearly 20,000 lb of thrust, slightly more than that generated by the A-10's engines.

Over seven per cent of the Su-25's normal take-off weight is taken up with built-in survivability measures. They include pushrod rather than cable-operated control surfaces and foam-lined, fire retardant fuel tanks.

Self-protection extends to a total of 256 flares packed into containers above the engine nacelles and the tailcone. These are routinely dispensed during attack runs, primarily to foil heat-seeking missiles.

needed for autonomous operation at airstrips providing only fuel and ammunition.

Other variants are the **Su-25UBK 'Frogfoot-C'** operational conversion trainer, and the **Su-28 'Frogfoot-D'** pure flying trainer with less powerful engines.

Specification
Sukhoi Su-25K 'Frogfoot-D'
Type: single-seat close support warplane
Powerplant: two 4500-kg (9,921-lb) thrust Tumanskii R-195 turbojets

Performance: maximum speed 850 km/h (528 mph), range 1100 km (684 miles)
Dimensions: span 14.36 m (47 ft 1.4 in); length 15.55 m (51 ft 0.2 in)
Weights: empty 9500 kg (20,944 lb); maximum take-off 17600 kg (38,801 lb)
Armament: one 30-mm cannon and up to 4500 kg (9,921 lb) of disposable stores
Users: Czech Republic, Hungary, Iraq, North Korea and Russian Federation.

As with the A-10, laser-guided bombs are standard equipment for Russian 'Frogfoot' squadrons. So accurate is the guidance system used that bombs can be placed within 16 ft of a target from 12 miles away.

HARRIER
The Mud Fighter

The Professional's View:

The Harrier GR.Mk 3

"It is a very good aeroplane; it seems to be able to survive battle damage well. Its small size and absence of smoke make it difficult for the enemy to see it coming, and the camouflage is effective. It is fast enough at low altitude – if you went much faster you wouldn't have time to pick out the targets. It's able to operate from absurdly small strips. It could do with a little more strengthening, armour plating around certain vital components like the fuel system and the pilot."

Harrier pilot

Some pilots believe that 'mud mover' ground-attack are no longer useful. But ask the men who won back the Falklands for their opinion of the Harrier. When support fire is needed only metres ahead of the advance, VTOL strike has the edge.

Two big flashes of fire show that the pilot of this Harrier has salvoed both loads of Matra rockets from quadruple pods under the wings. Each rocket has its own fire in the tail, which burns as long as it is in the air en route to the target. Harriers can carry relativelyfew different types of stores so accuracy is paramount.

Stealth means life in battle. If the enemy knows where you are, he can destroy you. Modern high-performance warplanes are potent beyond the imaginations of only a generation ago, but on Europe's Central Front they have one enormous handicap. They need air bases with long, concrete runways.

No matter how you camouflage your airfield, the enemy knows that if he destroys those runways all the multi-million-dollar fighting machines on the base are so much scrap metal. Which is why the unique capabilities of the Harrier 'jump-jet' make it one of the world's most useful attack aircraft.

Britain's pioneering vertical take-off and landing fighter has freed the tactical aircraft from the tyranny of the runway. Using hastily erected camouflaged hides on unprepared sites right behind the front line, it can operate from temporary airstrips or short, straight stretches of road. This ability to provide the closest of close support is what attracted the US Marine Corps into also buying the Harrier.

Once in the air, the transition to full wing-borne flight is rapid. Fast and agile at low level, the Harrier is supremely suited to the fiercely contested airspace above the modern battlefield.

Into the forests

At the first sign of hostilities, Harrier squadrons disappear into the field. They could be based in a forest, or a factory. They could be hidden in an out-of-town hypermarket or in a city bus-station. If the enemy gets too close, then the whole operation can be on the move within an hour and be back in action from a different location three hours later.

Falklands success

The Harrier's combat debut came in 1982. It was the outstanding success of the Falklands campaign. Operating in often atrocious conditions, the naval variant of the Harrier proved to be a ferocious dogfighter. RAF Harriers were used to attack Argentine ground targets, and maintained high serviceability operating from a variety of platforms and temporary airstrips. Indeed, were it not for the Harrier and Sea Harrier the British Task Force would not have been able to retake the islands.

Although its capabilities make it unique, the Harrier has always been hampered by its lack of range, relatively small weapons load and primitive avionics. The AV-8B Harrier II, developed by McDonnell Douglas and British Aerospace, is the answer to the Harrier pilot's prayer. Keeping all the versatility of the older design, the Harrier II carries more weaponry over longer distances, and state-of-the-art electronics fit it for the battlefields of the 1990s.

Soviet-beater

After more than 20 years, the Harrier remains a uniquely capable aircraft. The Soviet Yak-38, with its separate lift engine, is a much less versatile machine. Surprisingly for an aircraft with such obvious advantages, serving with the RAF, the Royal Navy and the US Marine Corps, the Harrier has not been sold elsewhere in large numbers. Only Spain (operating AV-8As and -Bs) and India (operating Sea Harriers) have joined the Harrier club, although interest in a naval variant is currently high in Italy and Japan.

Above: A Marine AV-8B comes in to land in a clearing close behind the front line. The US Marine Corps sees the Harrier as the ideal machine to fill its requirement for an aircraft able to give the closest of close support from temporary bases right in the middle of the battle.

1 Engine running at 55% RPM; Pilot runs pre-takeoff checks of fuel, armament master switches, flaps, jet nozzles. Nozzles are set to 10° for rough field Short Take Off (STO).

2 Pilot slams throttle to full power, releases brakes and accelerates forwards. Take-off speed has been calculated before take-off; cockpit display indicates when it is reached. Take-off roll with warload can be little more than 300 metres.

3 At STO speed, typically 80 or 90 knots, pilot slams nozzles to 55°, which automatically deploys the flaps. Combination of vertical lift from wings and jet nozzles lifts Harrier off the ground.

Falklands multi-role warrior

Sea Harriers and Sea King helicopters crowd the decks of a British carrier. HMS Hermes and Invincible each carried up to a dozen of the fighters to the South Atlantic.

Harriers and Sea Harriers received their baptism of fire in the 1982 operation to retake the Falklands. It was the first major naval action of the missile age, and many people were unsure as to how effective the fighter would be.

As the Task Force sailed south to the Falklands, the Royal Navy's Sea Harriers were kept busy. Argentina's long-range aircraft, including airliners and C-130 transport aircraft, had to be kept clear of the British Force by regular CAPs (combat air patrols).

If the operation were to succeed, the Argentines had to be denied the use of the airfield at Port Stanley. Task Force Sea Harriers made their first strike, using high explosive and cluster bombs to wreck the airfield facilities after RAF Vulcans had bombed the runway, making it unusable to Argentine fighters.

Sea Harriers demonstrated their multi-role capability by flying photo-reconnaissance missions over the Falklands to assess the effects of the bombing, and to check on the dispositions of Argentine troops.

Reaction to the attack was rapid, and Argentine aircraft made a number of attacks on the British ships. Sea Harriers

Short take-off

The Harrier is the world's only land-based STOVL (Short Take Off Vertical Landing) fighter. It takes off using vectored thrust, the pilot being able to point the aircraft's jet nozzles downwards as well as backwards. By doing this at the right moment he can take off in a fraction of the usual distance carrying the same weapon load. The sequence below shows the various stages a Harrier pilot goes through to get his warplane airborne.

5 Harrier accelerates away at 10 Alpha (10° Angle of Attack). Pilot moves nozzles aft over next 10 to 15 seconds, making smooth transition to wing-borne flight. As nozzles go back, flaps are automatically retracted.

6 Once in the air, the Harrier is just like any other jet fighter, though its small size and powerful engine give it exceptional manoeuvrability, especially at the low flight levels for which it was designed.

4 As Harrier lifts from the ground, pilot controls aircraft attitude using control stick, linked to reaction 'puffers' at nose, tail and on wingtips.

Extra lift from ground effect

The hot jet gases from the thrust-vectoring nozzles strike the surface and bounce back up onto the under-side of the jet.

When hovering and at low speed, normal control surfaces have no effect, so Harrier's attitude is controlled by small 'puffers', compressed air jets at nose, tail and on the wingtips.

By trapping these extra gases, the Harrier considerably increases its lift and payload.

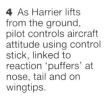

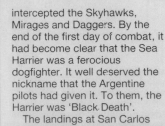

Left: A Sidewinder detonates against an Argentine fighter. Commander 'Sharkey' Ward scored three of the 21 kills by Sea Harriers during the Falklands war.

with the Task Force and landing on the carriers without difficulty.

As the land battle progressed, temporary landing sites were set up on the islands. This brought the Harriers much closer to the action, and they attacked Argentine positions with laser-guided bombs.

With the Harrier, British forces were able to achieve a momentous victory in the South Atlantic.

Below: RAF Harrier GR.Mk 3s arrived on the scene later than the Sea Harriers and specialised in ground attacks.

intercepted the Skyhawks, Mirages and Daggers. By the end of the first day of combat, it had become clear that the Sea Harrier was a ferocious dogfighter. It well deserved the nickname that the Argentine pilots had given it. To them, the Harrier was 'Black Death'.

The landings at San Carlos saw the RAF's Harrier GR.Mk 3s in action. Most had come south with the task force, but four had made an epic flight from Ascension Island, meeting up

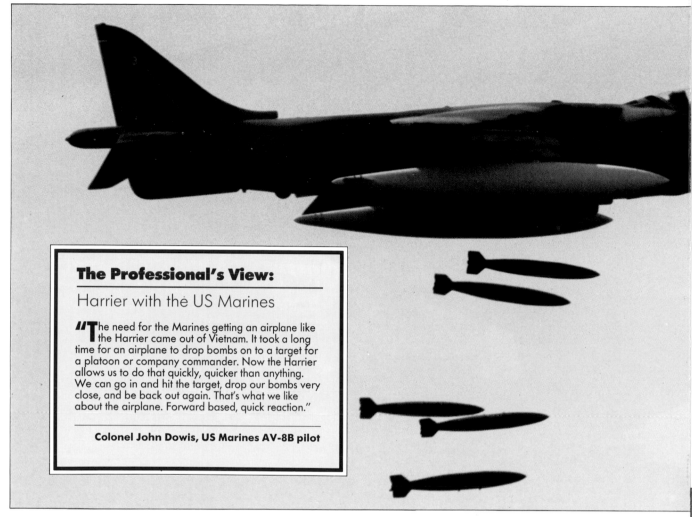

The Professional's View:

Harrier with the US Marines

"The need for the Marines getting an airplane like the Harrier came out of Vietnam. It took a long time for an airplane to drop bombs on to a target for a platoon or company commander. Now the Harrier allows us to do that quickly, quicker than anything. We can go in and hit the target, drop our bombs very close, and be back out again. That's what we like about the airplane. Forward based, quick reaction."

Colonel John Dowis, US Marines AV-8B pilot

The Harrier II is a systems aeroplane, much more than the original Harrier. Sophisticated avionics make it easier to fly and much more accurate in the attack missions for which it is tasked.

Above: The Harrier II can carry twice as much as the original Harrier, or the same load over greater distances. This Marine Corps AV-8B is dropping 1,000-lb low-drag high-explosive bombs.

Right: The AV-8B can carry a variety of stores, including (front to back) Sidewinder air-to-air missiles, air-to-ground rockets, fuel-air explosives, cluster bombs and a range of conventional bombs.

LASER-GUIDED BOMBS

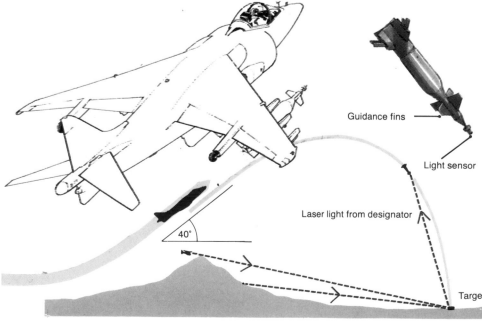

Guidance fins

Light sensor

Laser light from designator

40°

Target

High technology has done wonders for bombing accuracy. Laser designation means that you can put a high-explosive bomb through the side window of a truck from six miles away. The procedure is simple. A designator, who can be on the ground or in a helicopter, shines the laser beam at the target. Laser energy is reflected from the target and is picked up by sensors in the nose of the Harrier and in the bomb. The plane's computer calculates the moment of release, usually in a climb, so the bomb is tossed high and forwards. The bomb's sensor homes in one the target, using nose and tail fins to alter its course.

LERX
Small wing
Root Exter
dramatical
radius by l
destabilisir
They also
wing rock
Much large
fitted to R/
part of the
programm

ATTACK TEAM

Even though the threat of war in Europe has diminished, the Joint Attack Team developed to kill Soviet tanks could still find itself in action from the Arctic to the Equator.

The main offensive elements of the joint air attack team are close air support aircraft (below) and attack helicopters (left below, inset). Their targets are hostile enemy armoured formations (main picture, left) which are crushed between the jaws of an attack made possible by modern anti-tank missiles, and carried out in a co-ordinated fashion. This means that the enemy is subjected to continuous assault from a number of different directions.

Above: The Fairchild A-10A Thunderbolt II is an extremely potent warplane. It is heavily armoured, capable of bearing a large weapons load and with an immensely powerful 30-mm cannon firing depleted uranium armour-piercing shells that can destroy any battle tank.

1 Recon at the Front

Above: Scout helicopters check out avenues of approach and suitable engagement areas, and locate enemy air defences for suppression before they engage the close-support aircraft.

To be effective in any sort of combat, you have to know where the enemy is. Combat requires intelligence of the enemy, and this can be acquired in a number of ways. Specialised reconnaissance units, in helicopters or light armoured vehicles, seek out and report on enemy movements. Ground troops in contact with the enemy report back to rear echelons. All information is collated and, if it seems a combined attack can set the enemy back, the Joint Attack Team is activated.

The Joint Attack Team is there to support the ground troops. These troops are very important, often being the first to report the presence of the enemy.

2 Artillery Bombardment

Artillery is first used on the instructions of a Forward Air Controller to slow the enemy attack, to suppress enemy air defence radars, to cause enemy armour to 'button up' (that is, to close all hatches against flying shell splinters) and so reduce their visibility, and to move on to suppress enemy follow-up forces as the air attack teams go in. Support can be from field artillery units, or from the guns of warships while within range of the coast. Artillery is also the main way of suppressing dismounted infantry.

Above: Artillery can assist the attack team by saturating advancing enemy columns with shells.

Right: Artillery is vital to the Joint Attack Team, being used to suppress enemy air defences and to disrupt dismounted infantry.

While helicopters wait in hiding, a forward observer in a scout helicopter will correct the artillery fire.

Artillery support can range from the small towed howitzer to the giant self-propelled 203-mm howitzer seen here.

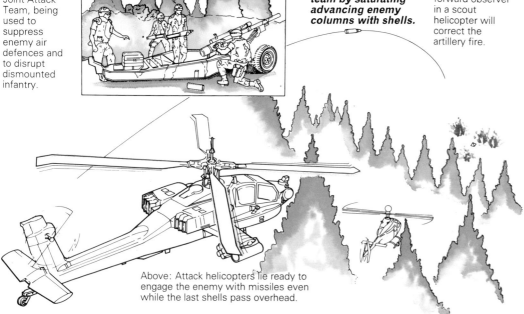

Above: Attack helicopters lie ready to engage the enemy with missiles even while the last shells pass overhead.

3 Helicopter Attack

Below: The US Army's Apache is armed with Hellfire missiles, able to engage tanks out to 6 km range.

As the artillery fire mission comes to an end, the Forward Air Controller calls in the attack helicopters that have been loitering in the trees. Popping up, they make their attack, firing at targets designated by scout helicopters or ground observers. After a pre-determined period, they pull back to allow the next phase of the attack to go in. The helicopters have the advantage of being able to engage at long range, and they can deal with air defence artillery previously identified by scout helicopters. Their attack is co-ordinated with artillery and close-support aircraft, allowing an enemy to be attacked repeatedly without pause.

Above: Modern helicopters can engage tanks or anti-aircraft vehicles at ranges of 4000 m or more, dipping back into hiding once they have released their missiles.

Below: The first targets to be designated by the scouts, and hence the first to be hit by missiles, should be enemy air defence weapons, as these can wreak havoc among attacking fighters.

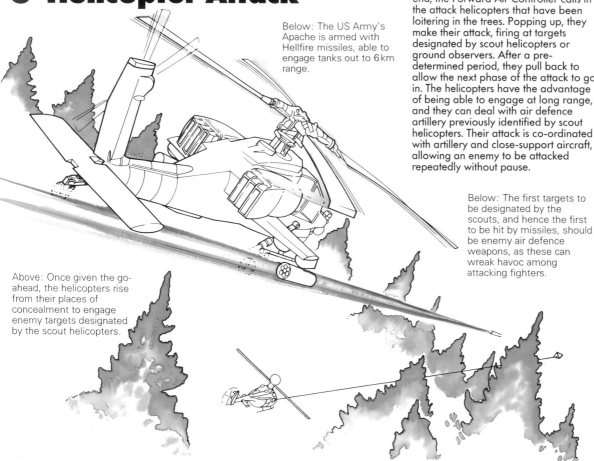

Above: Once given the go-ahead, the helicopters rise from their places of concealment to engage enemy targets designated by the scout helicopters.

4 A-10 into Action

Below: The A-10 has a variety of weapons it can use on tanks, ranging from Maverick missiles with a range of up to 25 km, through the gun with a range of 3000 m, to simple 'iron' bombs, which necessitate passing over the target.

As the helicopters redeploy to new firing positions, the Forward Air Controller designates targets for the close air support aircraft. Typically, aircraft such as the Fairchild A-10, a heavily armed and armoured bruiser, will attack with Maverick missiles and guns. Smart weapons can also be carried, their targets designated by the same assets that have done the job for the attack helicopters. The aircraft and helicopters continue to sequence into and out of the target area until the target is destroyed or until fuel and ammunition is low.

The tactics used by A-10s vary depending on the weapons used. The gun is fired from a sharp, jinking approach, while bombs require a straighter line. Once the attack is made the aircraft turns sharply away to make room for the next artillery or helicopter attack.

Below: The essence of the Joint Attack Team is continuous assault. The helicopters are warned when the A-10s are making their run, so they can sink down out of sight.

Below: Stealth is the helicopter's greatest merit. From its hide, it can get into action within seconds of an artillery bombardment or an aircraft attack.

Above: Clumsy and ungainly though it may be, the A-10 is highly manoeuvrable at low speeds and very low altitudes.

Below: The purpose of the Joint Attack Team is to make sure it is a ground target that blows up, not one of your aircraft.

Above: The trail of smoke from a burst of bottle-sized 30-mm rounds is the only visual indication that the most powerful aircraft gun in the world is firing. The A-10's GAU-8 cannon can fire armour-piercing rounds weighing half a kilogram at up to 70 rounds per second.

Left: Powerful though it is, the gun is not the only weapon the A-10 uses. Here a Thunderbird lays down 227-kg (500-lb) retarded bombs during a low pass over the target.

PHANTOM
Support

EYE WITNESS

"My return to Vietnam was anything but triumphant. Whereas before I had been imbued with purpose, now I felt a deeper detachment. Before, I had been essentially childlike in my love of flying; now I was a precision instrument of destruction to whom flying was an unquestioned but minor skill. I was the weapons system, with a 25-ton monster as an extension of my will."

Major John Trotti, US Marine Corps

EYE WITNESS

"My return to Vietnam was anything but triumphant. Whereas before I had been imbued with purpose, now I felt a deeper detachment. Before, I had been essentially childlike in my love of flying; now I was a precision instrument of destruction to whom flying was an unquestioned but minor skill. I was the weapons system, with a 25-ton monster as an extension of my will."

Major John Trotti, US Marine Corps

F-4J Phantom, US Marine Corps

The F-4J had more powerful engines than the F-4B and also had an improved bombing system. This was important, as marines used their F-4s for ground attack more than any other user.

Above: Marines under fire north of Da Nang crouch behind a paddy field dyke as an F-4 Phantom roars overhead to lay its ordnance onto the ambushers of the North Vietnamese Army.

Weapons control
The F-4J was fitted with a Lear-Siegler AJB-7 bombing system, giving the aircraft full air-to-ground capacity. This computes the correct moment for weapons release, taking into account speed, height, aircraft attitude, and angle to target.

Below: Bomb- and rocket-armed Phantoms from VMFA-542 head for the Vietnamese Demilitarised Zone on a ground support mission.

Marine Air's main task is to support the 'Grunt', and Vietnam Phantoms dropped a lot of ordnance doing just that.

EYE WITNESS

"We spotted an NVA soldier between Hills 881N and 881S. We contacted the 60-mm mortars, who marked the enemy's position by dropping white phosphorus to within 50 metres of him. Through the scope we could see him set to with his entrenching tool, speeding up when he heard the jets we'd called. One of the jets dropped two 250-lb bombs right on him. I could see the guy go up with the bomb cloud. We gave the pilots 'one confirmed', and the grunts around us cheered."

Tactical Air Controller, Khe Sanh

John Trotti was a Marine Corps F-4 Phantom pilot in Vietnam. In his two tours of duty he did everything from dodging the dreaded SAMs while on bombing missions over North Vietnam to sitting at instant readiness on the 'Hot Pad', ready for immediate action in support of fellow Marines in trouble on the ground. In 1969, he was just starting his second tour and after cooling his heels on administrative tasks for some weeks had at last been assigned to a squadron at Chu Lai.

Pinned down

"I was at the squadron operations office before seven, eager to begin checking in, only to be asked if I wanted to stand the Hot Pad. Absolutely, because if anything interesting was going to happen, that's where it would be. Ten minutes after I arrived at the Hot Pad van, the duty officer's phone went off, and I was on my way. There was a reconnaissance patrol of 15 men pinned down by two companies of NVA near Khe Sanh, so 'A' Pad scrambled with Dan Martin on my wing and Skip Sines in my back seat. The weather was fine at Chu Lai, but north of Da Nang we picked up a cloud layer that thickened the farther we went, until it extended from a few hundred feet above the ground to more than 6,000 feet, obscuring not only the enemy positions but the surrounding mountains as well.

Bad news

"Although we couldn't talk directly with the men on the ground, we could relay messages back and forth through the leader of the rescue helicopter flight hovering in the clear, awaiting a chance to extract the patrol. The news was not good. The patrol had already taken heavy casualties with three dead and six wounded, three seriously. The NVA units were above them in prepared positions with fields of fire choking off escape by foot and preventing helicopter evacuation. The choppers couldn't go in until the patrol moved several hundred yards farther into the valley.

"We let down underneath the overcast over the coastal plain, popping out at 500 feet near the entrance to the valley on a north-westerly heading. Some of the hills went up to 7,000 feet and there were smaller outcroppings that didn't register on the maps. Typical of the weather at that time of the year, the bases of the clouds were ragged along the hills, so that only in the centre of the valley was there room to manoeuvre.

No room to manoeuvre

"Leaving Dan over the flatland, I worked myself up to the end of the valley where the fighting was taking place. From the description the choppers had given, I could make out where the friendlies were, but we ran out of manoeuvring room before we could find (much less drop on) the enemy positions. Reaching the end of the valley, I had to light the afterburners and climb straight up through the clouds to avoid the unseen hills – the ubiquitous 'cumulo granite.' It was frustrating to be in the area with the right ordnance just when it was really needed and not be able to do anything to help. I was about to call Joyride to see if they could arrange for naval gunfire support when the lead rescue chopper came on the line.

Dummy runs

"'Keep it up, Asp. Recce Six says that you came right over the top of the enemy position and got their attention. They stopped firing for nearly a minute.'

"'Relay to Recce that I didn't see a thing, but I'll keep making dummy runs to keep them down

Performance
The Phantom added a new dimension to carrier-based air power. Capable of a speed of more than 1,290 knots (2390 km/h; 1,350 mph) at altitude, a more typical operating speed when loaded up with external ordnance would be 520 knots (965 km/h; 600 mph).

Weapons load
Although a Phantom can carry six tons of bombs, a typical combat load in Vietnam would be six Mk 83 750-lb (340-kg) low-drag bombs and unguided folding-fin air-launched rockets in pods beneath the wing.

Above: Navy Phantoms also provided Grunt support, though their main tasks were in the hostile skies of the North.

Above: Da Nang was one of the busiest airfields in South East Asia, and was home base to a large number of Marine F-4s.

until the clouds lift.'

"During the next 15 minutes we made half a dozen passes, each time allowing the recon patrol to withdraw a few yards, but the clouds showed no signs of lifting. Fuel was beginning to be a concern, and Skip, who had arrived overseas just that week and had never been exposed to the madness of continually punching up and down through the clouds, was getting panicky.

Nerves in the back seat

"At first his protestations were mildly irritating, but after a while he got to me. Why anyone would volunteer for the rear seat is a mystery, but once there, it was his job to stick it out. This was the first time I had had a serious concern that an RIO might just punch out, and he was so out of control that I told him make sure that his ejection select switch was in the 'rear seat only' position so that I wouldn't get lofted into the boonies if he followed through with his threats. Finally I'd had enough and ordered him to shut up, unplug his microphone, or go the hell on and punch out, whichever suited him best.

"'Asp, Recce Six reports that the unfriendlies are moving out of their positions and readying for an attack.' That was what I had been afraid of. We had made a bunch of runs and failed to drop, so it was only a matter of time before they got the idea that we were a paper tiger.

"'You'd better ask Recce if things are bad enough that he's willing for me to drop over the top

of him. Tell him to mark his farthest forward position with red smoke.'

"'Roger, Asp, Red smoke on its way. He says, "Sock it to 'em".'

"Any run in the hills is hard enough, but in this case we were stuck with releasing horizontally, or perhaps even in a slight climb, in order to reach the enemy position on the hillside with the bombs. There just wasn't any gunsight setting for releasing Snakeyes that took this into account, so it was going to be 'wing it' time.

"'OK, Dash Two, I'm setting up 210 mils for a level 450-knot delivery. Give me a 45-second interval and if my hits are confirmed and if you have everybody's smoke, go and drop. Otherwise abort it high and dry.'

Clouds lifted

"With a grim determination, I plunged once again through the clouds and into the valley, only to be greeted by an amazing sight. The clouds had lifted as if by magic, and I could see the plume of red fully five miles away. Rocketing by Asp Two, I reset my gunsight for a 10-degree delivery, selected *cluster, all*, nose and tail *arm*, and master arm *on*.

"'Ask Recce how many metres forward of the smoke the gooners are. I'll be on target in 30 seconds."

"'They're 12 o'clock for 100 metres in the open! Waste 'em!'

"Rolling inverted with the belly of the airplane scrubbing the clouds, we ripped over the top of the recon team. Pulling the nose below the horizon, I planted my sight on a point a football field's length beyond the smoke and corkscrewed back to the upright, boring in until everything but the spot beneath the pipper was a blur. Just at the instant of release I saw a swirl of movement where the bombs were aimed, and then I was off into the clouds.

"'Outstanding! OUTSTANDING! Right on the mark. Dash Two, put yours right on top of Dash One's smoke.

"Another flight followed in behind us, but it wasn't necessary. The enemy had ceased firing, allowing the recon patrol to withdraw into the valley for pickup by the choppers.

Eight out

"'Cheer up, Skip, we've got two more hours on the pad when we get back.' But he wasn't consumed with enthusiasm, opting instead to go to sick bay.

"That night I got a phone call in my hootch.

'Hello, Asp, this is Recce Six. I just wanted you to know that we

got out with eight troops. We had to leave seven, but we're going back tomorrow to bring their bodies out. I'll try to get a KBA on the dinks while we're up there. Come up to Quang Tri and we'll do the town.'

"I felt good to have done something of value – all the more so because it hadn't been easy. I called Skip over to cheer him up, and Dan and his RIO, and after several toasts to the guts of the Force Recon people, I proposed that the first chance I got to fly the Hummer up to Quang Tri, we would go up there and accept their hospitality.

"We never got the chance. After the close call, you'd have thought Recce Six lived a charmed life, but luck no less than fame is an illusion. Though we didn't learn of it until several weeks later, he died the next day when the rappelling line parted as he dangled over the jungle at a hundred feet during helicopter extraction. At least he had the extra day, which may seem small for all the effort, but I'd still take the Hot Pad for lesser triumphs than that."

BIG BOMBERS

Symbol of flexible power, the bomber has been a symbol of air power for 80 years. Defender of peace and conveyor of war, its presence continues with new shapes and new 'magic powers'.

"We coasted in north-west of Haiphong and headed for our Initial Point, where we would turn south-west towards Hanoi. The flak started coming up when we made our first landfall. Once again we were most vividly aware of the heavy, black, ugly explosions that characterised the 100-mm. Even at night, the black smoke from these explosions is visible.

"We picked up the first signals from incoming SAMs. We could see them lifting off, but their guidance seemed erratic and they exploded far above us. However, inbound to the target the SAM signals became stronger. The aircraft commander ordered the cell of B-52s

Crew of a B-52 keep formation on a bombing raid over Vietnam. Strategic Air Command conducted 126,000 such bombing sorties during that war and dropped more bombs (over 6 billion pounds) than all those used in World War II.

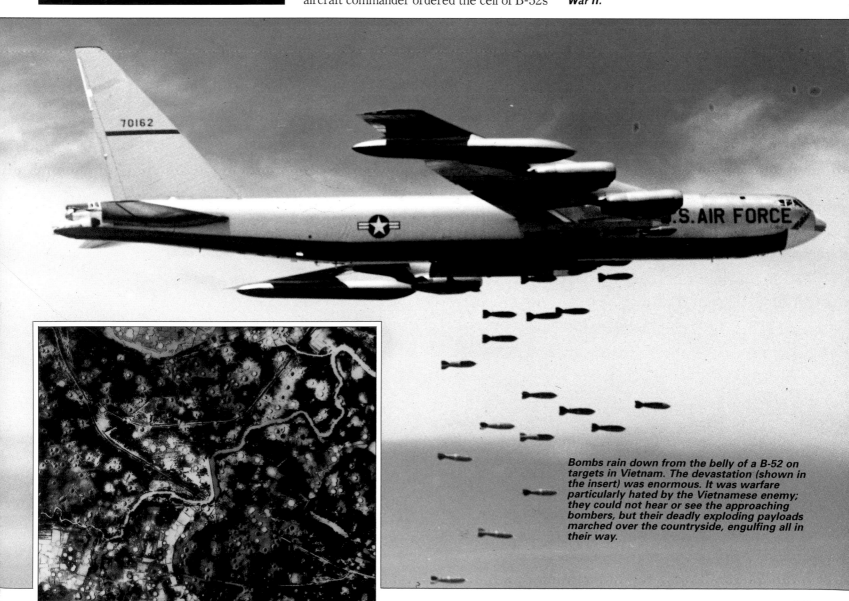

70162

U.S. AIR FORCE

Bombs rain down from the belly of a B-52 on targets in Vietnam. The devastation (shown in the insert) was enormous. It was warfare particularly hated by the Vietnamese enemy; they could not hear or see the approaching bombers, but their deadly exploding payloads marched over the countryside, engulfing all in their way.

153

to start SAM threat manoeuvres. Then they really started coming.

"Now the whole force was committed to the bomb run. I decided to count the SAMs launched against us. About 100 seconds prior to bombs away, the cockpit lit up like it was daylight. The light came from the rocket exhaust of a SAM that had come up right under our nose. That one looked like it missed us by less than 50 feet.

Fireworks factory

"After 25 SAMs, I quit counting. At bombs away, it looked like we were right in the middle of a fireworks factory that was in the process of blowing up."

That was what it was like during the operation known as Linebacker II over North Viet-

With a wing severed by an enemy fighter, a B-17 spirals down over Germany.

Rain of destruction

Bombing was the one way that Britain and America could strike back at Germany while they prepared for their ultimate invasion of Europe. At first they got off to a difficult start. Early missions would see over half the aircraft destroyed, but as formation tactics and fighter cover improved bombers pushed further and further into the German heartland, where formations of up to 1,000 bombers inflicted crippling damage.

The hapless citizens of Tokyo take delivery of yet more ordnance from a formation of B-29s. it was this type that dropped the first atom bombs on Hiroshima and Nagasaki, although their previous 'conventional' raids killed far more people than those two nuclear explosions.

nam in December 1972, the 11-day campaign that ended the US involvement in Vietnam and brought about a ceasefire.

Down in South Vietnam the eight-engined B-52 had earlier been a tactical bomber. It flew so high on hundreds of 'Arc Light' sorties that it couldn't be seen or heard. The first the enemy knew about it was when the jungle blew up. Five, 10, 20, 100 times the earth trembled as the bombs exploded. Hugging the ground, Viet Cong guerrillas could only wait until the holocaust of steel and fire had passed – until the next time the tactical Stratofort, the 'big stick', paid them a visit.

The B-52 had become the most important bomber of the US Strategic Air Command. After World War II, the Cold War between the West and Russia threatened to get hotter by the week, and if 'Round Three' broke out with a pre-emptive Soviet missile or bomber strike, SAC would have evened the score by using this eight-jet aircraft with its huge bombload and outstanding range.

BIG BOMBERS Reference File

107

USA 🇺🇸

Rockwell B-1B

The **B-1B** entered service in 1986 as replacement for the B-52, and is a capable warplane despite continued problems with the defensive electronics. The origins of the type lie with a 1969 requirement for a high-altitude bomber with Mach 2.2+ dash capability. The resulting swing-wing B-1A first flew in 1974, but in 1977 the project was cancelled by President Carter.

In 1981 President Reagan revived this bomber in the form of the B-1B optimised for the low-level role at high subsonic speeds. The airframe and landing gear remained comparatively unchanged apart from structural strengthening, but the powerplant was considerably revised with modified

nacelles and fixed rather than variable-geometry inlets for a maximum speed cut back to Mach 1.25. Other modifications included the incorporation of radar-absorbent materials in certain parts of the airframe to lessen the type's radar signature, already reduced significantly by the installation of S-shaped ducts in the inlets with baffles to shield the faces of the engine compressors.

Specification
Rockwell B-1B
Type: four-seat strategic heavy bomber and missile-carrying warplane
Powerplant: four 13962-kg (30,780-lb) thrust General Electric F101-GE-102 turbofans

Performance: maximum speed 1330 km/h (825 mph); range 10380 km (6,450 miles)
Dimensions: span 41.67 m (136 ft 8.5 in) spread and 23.84 m (78 ft 2.5 in) swept; length 44.81 m (147 ft 0 in)
Weights: empty 87091 kg (192,000 lb); maximum take-off 216367 kg

(477,000 lb)
Armament: up to 29030 kg (64,000 lb) of free-fall bombs or missiles (AGM-69A SRAM-A, AGM-86B ALCM, AGM-129A ACM and AGM-131A SRAM-II) carried internally and externally
User: USA

When the prototype B-52 flew in April 1952, SAC knew it had a winner. In time, most of the 744 B-52s built saw service with more than 65 USAF combat wings, and in 1990 updated G and H models still formed an impressive "Oh, no, you don't" fleet of 261 dispersed around the USA.

2,600-bomber fleet

That a nuclear war did not happen was partly due to US strength in the bomber field. The Americans once had 2,600 bombers ready to attack targets 4,000 miles distant with full loads of conventional and, if necessary, nuclear bombs. Any aggressor knew the amount of destruction that retaliation by SAC's biggest would bring. And so far, the superpower bombers have only had to train for war.

After World War II, when the bomber fleets of Britain and the US that had poured

Britain was the third country to explode an atom bomb and three new jet bombers – the V-bombers – were built to deliver it. In the foreground is the Valiant, the first of the new breed. The delta-winged Vulcan leads the formation and is flanked by the Victor.

bombs down on the hapless cities of Germany and Japan were melted down for scrap, the world was supposed to be at peace. It wasn't, really. Small conflicts broke out, and in 1950 the Korean war caught the United Nations off balance at first.

Very soon, bombers were needed to hit bridges, factories and rail lines in North Korea to stop a communist offensive taking over the entire country. Round two for the B-29, the veteran of the bombing of Japan, was tough. But it did good work, despite taking losses from flak and fighter attack, including the slashing cannon fire of the MiG-15 jet.

With the Korean armistice, the US bomber force was rapidly converted to jets when the

six-engined B-47 Stratojet became an elegant SAC peacekeeper. It had taken over from a developed Superfortress known as the B-50, and the giant 10-engined Convair B-36, the 'aluminium overcast' that held the line for years and ably bridged the prop and jet eras.

Britain also needed big aircraft with the range, fuel load and engine power to deliver her 'ultimate weapon' to the Soviet heartland if necessary. So were born the V-bombers, the Valiant, Vulcan and Victor, a long-awaited trio after the propeller-driven Lincoln had soldiered on until the mid-1950s.

Most of the bombers of the 1950s and 1960s dropped nuclear weapons and free-fall bombs, but only to see how well they worked. Enormous mushroom clouds over remote Pacific islands answered that question. Nobody but a madman would have sparked off a real war with such destruction under a bomb-aimer's thumb.

108
Boeing B-52 Stratofortress

USA

The B-52 entered service in 1955 as a high-altitude bomber, but was transformed into a low-altitude type from 1962. The two surviving variants are the **B-52G** and **B-52H** (167 and 95 respectively out of 193 and 102 aircraft).

The B-52G that first flew in 1958 introduced integral wing tankage, two fixed underwing tanks and a broad-chord tail with remotely controlled rather than manned tail turret. The B-52H first flew in 1961 as carrier for the later-cancelled AGM-87 Skybolt missile, and introduced 7711-kg (17,000-lb) thrust Pratt & Whitney TF33-P-3 turbofans and a 20-mm tail cannon.

Both types have been very considerably upgraded in their offensive and defensive electronics, and whilst

they are still able to deliver free-fall conventional and nuclear weapons they have been modernised with a primary armament of nuclear-tipped missiles. The B-52G can carry 12 AGM-86B air-launched cruise missiles or 20 AGM-69A SRAM-A defence-suppression missiles, while the B-52H can carry up to 20 AGM-86Bs as the bomb bay has been modified to carry the eight-round Common Strategic Rotary Launcher.

Specification
Boeing B-52G Stratofortress
Type: six-seat strategic heavy bomber and missile-carrying warplane
Powerplant: eight 6237-kg (13,750-lb)

thrust Pratt & Whitney J57-P-43WB turbojets
Performance: maximum speed 957 km/h (595 mph); range 12070+ km (7,500+ miles)
Dimensions: span 56.39 m (185 ft 0 in); length 49.05 m (160 ft 10.9 in)
Weights: empty not revealed;

maximum take-off 221357+ kg (488,000+ lb)
Armament: four 12.7-mm (0.5-in) machine-guns in the tail turret and up to 22680 kg (50,000 lb) of disposable stores carried internally and externally
User: USA

To ensure their defence, the Russians developed many long-range bombers and today they have a formidable arsenal. It includes the Tupolev Tu-160, a swing-wing design similar to the American B-1 with the NATO codename 'Blackjack'; the Tu-22 'Blinder'; Tu-26

'Backfire'; the giant turboprop Tu-142 'Bear' and the Tu-16 'Badger'. Most of these would be used to attack targets in the West if war broke out or to provide all-important electronic surveillance and reconnaissance.

Western bombers have occasionally been

Dwarfing the previously-giant B-29 bomber, the massive 10-engined B-36 could stay aloft for nearly 24 hours, had a range of 8,000 miles and could range over China and Russia, constantly threatening nuclear devastation. It was so large that they even tested hooking up its own fighter for protection.

109

Northrop B-2

USA

The **B-2** is an extremely bold attempt to produce a strategic bomber with sufficient 'stealth' to avoid detection by an enemy's electro-magnetic and infra-red sensors except at very close range, and thus to restore the bomber's capability for medium-altitude cruise with all its advantages in range and reduced crew fatigue. Thus the design of the internal structure and curvaceous external surface is optimised to dissipate or trap radar energy rather than reflect it, while the installation of non-afterburning turbofans mixes hot exhaust gases with cold freestream air before release through the two-dimensional nozzles to reduce both thermal and acoustic signatures.

First flown in July 1989, the B-2 uses

a high proportion of composite materials in its structure, and in design is a flying wing with the leading edges swept at 40° and the trailing edges arranged in a W-layout with simple control surfaces. There are no vertical surfaces, and emitting sensors have been reduced to an absolute minimum.

The B-2 entered service in 1994 with the 509th Bomb Wing at Whiteman AFB in Arizona. The planned procurement of 132 aircraft has been reduced to 20, with a unit cost of $1 billion.

Specification
Northrop B-2
Type: two/three-seat strategic heavy bomber and missile-carrying warplane

Powerplant: four 8618-kg (19,000-lb) thrust General Electric F118-GE-100 turbofans
Performance: maximum speed 764 km/h (475 mph); range 12230 km (6,800 miles)
Dimensions: span 54.43 m (172 ft 0 in); length 21.03 m (69 ft 0 in)

Weights: empty not revealed; maximum take-off 168286 kg (371,000 lb)
Armament: up to 36515 kg (80,500 lb) of disposable stores carried internally
User: USA

110

Tupolev Tu-160 'Blackjack'

FORMER USSR

First flown in 1982 for a service debut in 1988, the **Tu-160 'Blackjack'** may be regarded as a counterpart to the USA's Rockwell B-1B. The two types are of basically similar swing-wing configuration, but the Russian bomber is about 30 per cent larger and heavier than the American warplane.

The type possesses an unrefuelled combat radius of 7300 km (4,536 miles) on the basis of subsonic cruise at high altitude, transonic penetration at low altitude, and supersonic attack and departure at high altitude. In-flight-refuelling capability enables the Tu-160 to undertake longer-range missions. The Tu-160 has a warload of 16500 kg (36,376 lb) carried in two

lower-fuselage weapon bays and on two hardpoints under the wing gloves. The type can carry conventional or nuclear free-fall bombs, but is generally associated with the subsonic AS-15 'Kent' cruise missile, and the supersonic AS-19 cruise missile.

As with so many former Soviet aircraft, serviceability has become the chief threat. The number of aircraft available for operational service is very limited.

Specification
Tupolev Tu-160 'Blackjack'
Type: four-seat strategic heavy bomber and missile-carrying warplane
Powerplant: four 23000-kg (50,705-

lb) thrust turbofans of unknown type
Performance: maximum speed 2230 km/h (1,386 mph); range 14600 km (9,072 miles)
Dimensions: span 55.5 m (182 ft 10.4 in) spread and 33.75 m (110 ft 9 in) swept; length 55.5 m (170 ft 10 in)
Weights: empty 118000 kg

(260,140 lb); maximum take-off 275000 kg (606,261 lb)
Armament: up to 16500 + kg (36,376 + lb) of disposable stores carried internally and externally
User: Russian Fed

called to duty, of course. When Britain stormed into Suez to keep the canal open in 1956, a few Valiant sorties were flown against Egyptian airfields. The Vulcan attack on Port Stanley in the 1982 Falklands war was the V-bomber swansong.

Superbomber

Sharing deterrence with ICBMs and atomic subs, bombers have managed to keep the 'balance of terror' steady. Years of service flying and practice alerts took their toll on the big bombers, and one by one they stood down or were turned over to other roles.

In America in 1959 a lot of hope was pinned on the B-58 Hustler, a 1,300-mph superbomber that carried its load in a streamlined fuselage pod. High cost ($30 million each) killed the B-58 after only two USAF wings equipped with it.

These days, the aged B-52 is still in service, along with the Rockwell B-1 and the

Awesome in its size and power, the Soviet Tupolev 'Bear' bomber has remained in business for 35 years. It started life as a free-fall nuclear bomber but now carries nuclear-tipped cruise missiles which can fly a further 1,750 miles at ultra low level. 'Bears' constantly practise penetrating UK and US air defences.

111

FORMER USSR

Tupolev Tu-95 and Tu-142 'Bear'

The **Tu-95 'Bear'** first flew in 1954 and entered service little more than a year later, and is a truly remarkable aeroplane with jet-type performance provided by the combination of swept flying surfaces and extremely powerful turboprops each driving massive contra-rotating propeller units.

The Russian air arm's strategic force is known as Long-Range Aviation, and this still operates a few aircraft. These are **'Bear-A'** bombers (with a payload of 20000 kg/44,092 lb of free-fall weapons) and **'Bear-B'** missile-carriers (with a payload of one AS-3 'Kangaroo' missile semi-recessed under the fuselage), many of them reworked to **'Bear-G'** standard with two AS-4 'Kitchen' missiles carried

under the wings. The LRA is also acquiring an increasing number of the **Tu-142 'Bear-H'** variant, which is a new-build type that entered production in the late 1980s. This has a number of design, engineering and equipment improvements over the Tu-95 for take-off at a maximum weight of 188000 kg (414,462 lb) with a heavier fuel load for greater range.

Specification
Tupolev Tu-95 'Bear-A'
Type: 10-seat strategic heavy bomber and missile-carrying warplane
Powerplant: four 11035-kW (14,800-shp) Kuznetsov NK-12MV turboprops
Performance: maximum speed

925 km/h (575 mph); range 14800 km (9,197 miles)
Dimensions: span 51.1 m (167 ft 7.75 in); length 47.5 m (155 ft 10 in)
Weights: empty 86000 kg (189,594 lb); maximum take-off 154200 kg (339,947 lb)
Armament: six 23-mm cannon (two

each in the tail turret and two barbettes) and up to 20000 kg (44,092 lb) of disposable ordnance carried internally (and externally in reworked aircraft)
User: USSR

112

FORMER USSR

Tupolev Tu-16 'Badger'

The **Tu-16 'Badger'** was one of the first jet-powered bombers, and first flew in 1952 as the Tu-88 prototype. When it entered service as a strategic medium bomber late in 1953 or early in 1954 the Tu-16 represented a truly remarkable achievement in terms of payload and performance (especially speed and range).

The Long-Range Aviation arm of the Russian air force still operates more than 275 Tu-16s, and though a sizeable proportion of this total is tasked with the inflight refuelling and ECM/Elint roles, there are still many **'Badger-A'** bombers in service with free-fall conventional and nuclear weapons. There are also some **'Badger-L'** aircraft, and these appear to be

'Badger-As' upgraded with a new chin radar. Some 240 of Naval Aviation's 400 'Badgers' are tasked with the strike role.

The Tu-16 is also the mainstay of the Chinese strategic bombing capability in the form of the **Xian H-6**, of which more than 100 are in service.

Assembly capability for this 'Badger-A' clone was being transferred when China and the USSR broke off relations in 1960, and the Chinese reverse-engineered the aeroplane and its engines as the H-6 and Wopen-8 respectively.

Specification
Tupolev Tu-16 'Badger-A'
Type: six-seat strategic medium bomber

Powerplant: two 9500-kg (20,944-lb) thrust Mikulin AM-3M turbojets
Performance: maximum speed 990 km/h (615 mph); range 5800 km (3,604 miles)
Dimensions: span 32.93 m (108 ft 0.5 in); length 36.25 m (118 ft 11.25 in)
Weights: empty 37200 kg (82,010 lb);

maximum take-off 75800 kg (167,708 lb)
Armament: seven 23-mm cannon (one fixed and two each in the tail turret and two barbettes) and up to 9000 kg (19,841 lb) of disposable stores carried internally
Users: China, Iraq and USSR

After 24 years as the mainstay of the British nuclear bombing force, the conventional bomber against the Argentine forces on the Falklands just before its retirement in 1982.

In the space of 70 years the bomber has been transformed — and has transformed warfare. No longer does war have to be fought out face to face on a small battlefield. Now every corner of the globe is under threat. These four landmark aircraft (drawn to scale) show the changing capability of the bomber now paving the way for the latest types: the B-1B and the B-2 stealth.

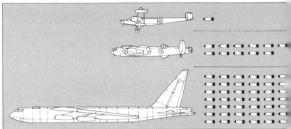

The diagram shows the growth of bombloads during the development of bombers. Each diagrammatical 'bomb' represents 2,000 lb, so in 24 years the Lancaster's load increased to 22,000 lb and about 15 years later the B-52 could carry 84,000 lb – 42 times that carried by the Handley Page O/400 in 1917.

1952 Avro Vulcan

One of three V-bombers designed to deliver the British nuclear bomb, the Vulcan could carry 21 1,000-lb conventional bombs or nuclear devices at 55,000 ft – for a time above the range of enemy air-to-air missiles. When enemy missiles became capable at this height, the Vulcan took to bombing at low level using the Blue Steel stand-off bomb to attack from a distance.

Northrop B-2 'Stealth', a flying wing that is all angles and corners so that it can't be picked up on enemy radar.

Cancelled in 1977, the B-1 was brought back four years later. The largest swing-wing design yet, it now serves four USAF combat wings and has a mostly low-level, under-the-radar strike role.

The amazing B-2, which has an estimated range of 6,600 miles carrying a weapons load exceeding 37,000 lb, costs no less than $500 million – for one aircraft! This is the main reason, in a more peaceful world, why the USAF order for B-2s will probably be reduced to about 75, but this in turn will take the unit cost up to $750 million. Maybe this Stealth design will be the last big bomber to be built: only time will tell.

The shape of things to come. The Northrop B-2 'stealth' bomber has been designed to attack targets without being seen by enemy radar. Built largely of composite fibre materials and formed into radar-absorbing or dissipating shapes, the B-2 shows up to be less than one thousandth the size of a normal bomber.

1952 Boeing B-52

Now the world's oldest serving bomber, the Stratofortress was flying long before many of its current crew members were born. Its mixture of bombload (12 nuclear bombs), operating height (55,000 ft) and range (12,500 miles) made the warplane an enduring symbol of Cold War terror.

the bomber

1917
Handley Page
O/400

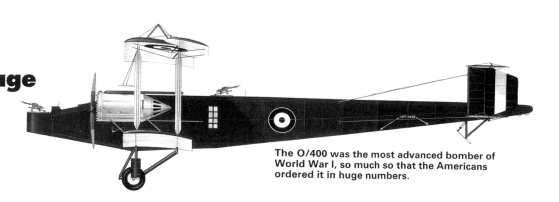

Built of wood, string and canvas, the O/400 was the world's first strategic bomber, designed to go beyond the front line of battle and to carry the war to the enemy's heartland. It was used against Germany during World War I.

The O/400 was the most advanced bomber of World War I, so much so that the Americans ordered it in huge numbers.

1941

Avro Lancaster

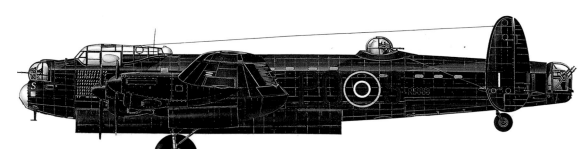

Backbone of the Royal Air Force bomber onslaught against Germany, the Lancaster brought new standards of bomb-carrying capacity at altitude. Normally it could carry 14,000 lb of bombs at 24,000 ft, but it was also able to drop a single 22,000-lb 'Grand Slam' monster against targets such as viaducts.

The Lancaster was an all-metal aircraft and could withstand tremendous punishment. It could deliver 132 tons of bombs for each aircraft lost compared with only 56 tons for earlier aircraft.

Above: Lancasters were used on specialised bombing missions such as the Dams raid, the sinking of the German battleship *Tirpitz* and the bombing of Hitler's retreat at Berchtesgaden.

Above: The huge delta wing of the Vulcan gave the type tremendous range and payload.

Above: Once they relinquished the strategic nuclear role, Vulcans went low-level and attacked targets in the same way as the Tornado does today.

Above: The large bulbous fairing at the rear of the aircraft was filled with electronic countermeasure equipment to shake off attacking missiles.

Below: This B-52 is painted in Vietnam warpaint. The 'Buff' was used to carpet-bomb the enemy in jungle hideouts and to support friendly troops when under attack at outposts such as Khe Sanh.

The B-52 was the aircraft used during the Linebacker raids when more than 150 bombers systematically bombed targets in North Vietnam during Christmas 1972. The campaign drove the North Vietnamese leaders to the negotiating table.

Keith Fretwell.

B-1B
The Penetrator

Sweeping around mountains or racing its shadow across a desert floor, it's all the same to the mighty Rockwell B-1. More projectile than flying machine, the deadliest bombers in the United States Air Force was built to hit the enemy with the most destructive weapons the world has ever known.

From nose tip to tail cone, the B-1B is 147 feet of power projection, dark-camouflaged to hide its sleek shape from high-flying enemy interceptors and missiles. But a modern bomber needs far more than paintwork to hide its mission. That's why the B-1 has 108 black boxes, aerials and jamming transmitters. They weigh 5,000 lb, as much as the entire bomb load of a World War II Flying Fortress.

These devices will ruin any enemy radar operator's day – all he would see would be electronic snow blotting out all his air defence screens. Meanwhile, the B-1B would be lining up on the target, seconds from 'bombs away'.

A typical penetration speed for the B-1 is around 640 knots, 200 feet above the ground. At that speed and height, a fighter would be bouncing around, banging the pilot's bonedome on the canopy roof. In the B-1, the ride is so smooth that you could write a letter.

Even if the enemy managed to 'see' the B-1 on radar, the electronic image would be reported as a small fighter, like the F-16. Rockwell engineers have so reduced the way radar waves bounce off the B-1's airframe that its true size simply can't be reproduced on the radar screen.

Swept-wing agility

A pilot and co-pilot control the B-1. Despite its size, it can be thrown around, particularly when the wings sweep back to just over 78 feet, down from nearly 137 feet fully spread. All this agile eagle needs to point it in the right direction is a fighter-like control stick.

So much importance is attached to the electronic counter measures fit of the B-1 that half the crew has this specialised task. One man handles the offensive ECM jammers, while the other can monitor any known radar frequency anywhere in the world. If anyone is trying to track the B-1, the crew will know.

Other changes have been made since the B-1 Penetrator first flew in December 1974. Then, it was seen as a high altitude nuclear attacker, but all that changed with new weapons that don't need a bomber to overfly the target at all.

Today, the B-1B is a Mach 1.25 stand-off bomber and cruise missile carrier in first-line service with Strategic Air Command at four main bases in the USA. It's one of the USAF 'big three' bombers, sharing the mission with the Northrop B-2 Stealth and the Boeing B-52. Together they represent an awesome challenge to any attacker.

The smooth contours of the B-1B give it some claim to being a 'stealth' bomber in its own right. It is thought to have a radar cross-section of about a quarter of that of the B-52.

Above: The tinted cockpit canopy of the B-1 slides under a tanker for air-to-air refuelling. Pilots rate this operation as very smooth, as the tanker's fuel boom clunks home three feet from the windscreen, making the job easy.

Left: Screaming to altitude, the B-1 dumps fuel from wingtip vents to lighten it for the climb. The bomber has a 'wet' wing, which indicates that that's where the tanks are. The sweeping curves of the airframe help hide the B-1's size on a radar screen.

Terrain-following bomb run

Terrain-following radar, one that looks down below the aircraft and senses hills, plains and valleys and automatically feeds altitude changes into the on-board computer, makes the B-1B the best 'mountaineer' in the world. When they're fully trained and able to sit there and let the invisible hands and feet fly the aircraft, crews marvel at how good this equipment is, making it all but impossible for the B-1 to run into anything.

Left: With wings swept, fighter-type manoeuvres are no problem even though the B-1B weighs 477,000 lb fully loaded, only 11,000 lb lighter than a B-52.

1 The B-1B can fly very low through mountainous or hilly terrain. It is equipped with forward- and downward-looking radar that projects a beam ahead of the aircraft.

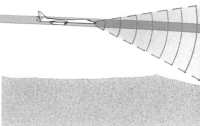

Electronic countermeasures

The heart of the B-1B's ECM capability is an Eaton system that searches for emissions from hostile radars. Powerful jamming equipment is then switched on by special crew operators who tune their sets to match the frequency of the radar trying to find the low-flying B-1. All the enemy will see is ground clutter, from hills and trees.

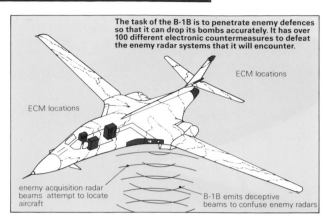

The task of the B-1B is to penetrate enemy defences so that it can drop its bombs accurately. It has over 100 different electronic countermeasures to defeat the enemy radar systems that it will encounter.

ECM locations

ECM locations

enemy acquisition radar beams attempt to locate aircraft

B-1B emits deceptive beams to confuse enemy radars

Below: Tail-warning radar and IFF – Identification Friend or Foe – aerials are built into the B-1B airframe, and they're purposely made hard to see. These tailplane panels (inset left) are about the only clue to the kind of capability this aircraft has.

3 Once clear of any obstruction, the radar return is once again uninterrupted and issues a 'pull-down' instruction. By making this calculation many times a second the terrain-following radar system enables the B-1B to hug the ground below at less than 250 ft.

2 A computer-generated 'ski-tip' shape is 'superimposed' onto the radar return. If this is interrupted by a return from the terrain below, it will issue a 'pull-up' instruction to the autopilot.

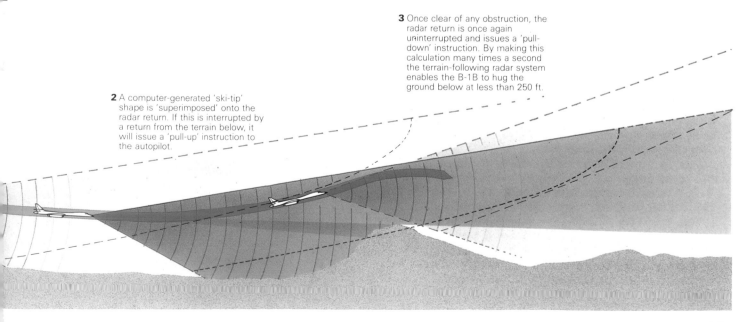

24 AGM-69
ge attack
l or B83
84,500-lb Mk
e bombs or
ix external
arry another

WEAPONS OF THE B-1B

Huge fleets of bombers are a thing of the past. For one thing, each one costs a fortune, and for another, aircraft like the B-1B are so capable that a lot of them are not really needed. Just one B-1B carries as much high explosive as the 'Big Belly' B-52s did over Vietnam. That's 84 500-lb 'iron' bombs.

Last resort

But the strictly strategic B-1B isn't ever likely to get involved in a 'limited' war like 'Nam. In a combat scenario, USAF chiefs would hold back the big swing-wing Rockwell until most other attack methods had been tried. If these failed, the B-1B might be called upon to finish the war with the biggest blast we've ever seen.

In its three internal weapons bays, the B-1B can carry, in a nuclear strike role, 24 SRAMs, 12 B28 or 24 B61 or B83 free-fall bombs. If the mission is non-nuclear the armourers can load in those 500-pounders to total a weight of 42,000lb.

Cruise missile load

The bomb bays will alternatively hold eight cruise missiles attached to a special Common Strategic Rotary Launcher, and if that's not enough and there are multiple targets that need taking out, the B-1B can take off with double cruise missiles on each of six pylons under the fuselage. This high number of cruise missiles per ship means that even two B-1Bs would give an enemy a 24-target headache!

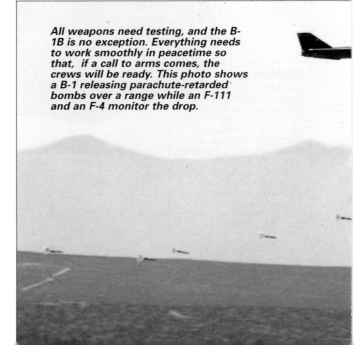

All weapons need testing, and the B-1B is no exception. Everything needs to work smoothly in peacetime so that, if a call to arms comes, the crews will be ready. This photo shows a B-1 releasing parachute-retarded bombs over a range while an F-111 and an F-4 monitor the drop.

B-52 TO TARGET

It first took to the air nearly 40 years ago; the examples flying today are older than the men who crew them. The threat it has to deal with is vastly more capable than it was in the 1950s. Yet the Boeing B-52 Stratofortress is still a vital part of America's strategic deterrent force.

Rumbling down the runway, all eight water-boosted Pratt & Whitney turbofan engines pumping out clouds of black smoke, the bomber labours to get into the air. It has a full fuel and missile load, taking it way beyond the weight at which it was designed to operate in the 1950s. Its huge wings flex alarmingly as they gain the lift that will take the giant aircraft into the sky. For the thousandth, or ten-thousandth time, a Boeing B-52 is off on operations.

The B-52 was designed in the aftermath of World War II, when the strategic bombing mission involved penetrating enemy airspace and dropping free-fall nuclear weapons from high altitude. This was fine, while defending fighters were not much quicker than the bombers they had to intercept. But the increasing sophistication of radar defences, the appearance of supersonic interceptors that could climb to the bomber's operating altitude in minutes, and, above all, the development of long-range surface-to-air missiles, meant that high-level bombing was tantamount to suicide.

The solution was to avoid the enemy's defences for as long as possible. If you don't register on radar, you don't alert those defences. And the only way to do that is to fly at very low level, beneath the radar coverage.

But the Stratofortress was designed as a high-altitude nuclear bomber. At low level, the B-52 is quite a handful. Its large size and the long wing, which was designed for high-altitude performance, are not at all suitable for dodging around among the treetops. Using the B-52 at low level calls for all the assistance that modern electronic systems can give.

Left: The B-52 is getting old, and its best chance of dealing with sophisticated modern air defences is to use long-range stand-off missiles. The AGM-86B air-launched cruise missile has a range of 2500 km, and the B-52 carries 12 on underwing pylons and a further eight in a rotary launcher in the bomb-bay.

1 Arming up

Good though it is, the B-52 cannot penetrate the most modern air defences with impunity. It's just too big, and lacks manoeuvrability. However, by using nuclear-tipped air-to-ground missiles you can attack from hundreds or even thousands of kilometres' distance. Since 1972, the main stand-off weapon for the B-52 has been the supersonic AGM-69 SRAM short-range attack missile. This has a range of 200 kilometres and carries a 170 kiloton warhead. The B-52 carries 20 SRAMs, eight in the bomb-bay and 12 on underwing pylons.

In the 1980s, the B-52 was the first carrier of the AGM-86B air-launched cruise missile (ALCM). This accurate missile has a high-subsonic performance, and a range of 2500 kilometres. The B-52G can carry 12 missiles and the B-52H can carry 18.

At the height of the Cold War the US strategic bomber force was dedicated to the nuclear role. The Vietnam War proved that a conventional bombing capacity was still vital, and the B-52 was adapted to carry the heaviest load of high explosive ever dropped by a bomber, becoming the eapon most feared by the communists. Since then, the huge bombers have acquired a third task, being configured for worldwide maritime strike using Harpoon anti-ship missiles.

Left: A B-52 prepares to refuel. The KC-135 tanker can pump nearly three tons of fuel per minute, and a complete refuelling can take 15 minutes.

Below left: The B-52 was originally intended to be propeller-driven, but the development of more efficient turbojets meant that it eventually appeared with eight Pratt & Whitney turbofans. The engines have to work hard to get a fully laden Stratofortress into the air, and on take-off the aircraft leaves a characteristic trail of dense smoke.

Above: When the B-52 was designed, strategic bombers dropped massive thermo-nuclear bombs from high altitude. Unfortunately, the development of modern air defences has made that strategy suicidal. Bombers are now expected to go in on the deck, although the sheer size of the B-52 means that it cannot fly as low as a tactical fighter.

2 Flying to target

B-52s cruise most efficiently at between 30,000 and 35,000 feet, although as a mission proceeds and fuel is burned an aircraft will drift closer to its service ceiling of 50,000 feet or more. At these altitudes, a B-52H has a range of some 16,000 kilometres. Low-level flight uses a lot of fuel, however, so the bomber must take on more from a Strategic Air Command KC-135 or KC-10 tanker before starting a low-level penetration. This refuelling normally takes place at altitudes above 27,000 feet.

3 Low-level penetration

Radar waves tend to travel in straight lines, just like sight. This means that if you fly high you will be above the horizon at a much greater distance than if you keep low. Low-level penetration requires an aircraft to fly just above the ground to get beneath the radar coverage. But low-level flight in a B-52 is tricky. You cannot jink and turn like a fighter: in a 40-degree bank the wing-tip is 55 feet closer to the ground than the fuselage. Chasing contours must be done with wings level.

4 Countering defences

The B-52 is packed with electronic countermeasures. These include radar warning receivers to detect enemy radar across the whole electronic spectrum; noise jammers that seek to overwhelm enemy radar signals; ECM generators that detect and analyse enemy radars in split-seconds, before sending almost identical signals on the same waveband, which appear on enemy screens as a false target well away from the real plane; and tail warning radars that identify and discriminate between approaching aircraft and missiles, and are range-sensitive so that when the enemy closes the bomber will automatically dispense chaff to jam enemy radar or flares to decoy enemy heat-seeking missiles. However, the easiest way to defeat enemy defences is to avoid being detected, and B-52s are equipped with a highly capable offensive avionics system, with accurate inertial navigation and terrain comparison systems that allow the bomber to weave its way through any of the enemy's defensive blind spots.

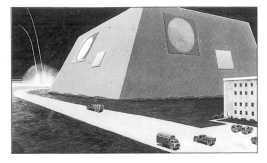

Above and right: in spite of incidents such as German teenager Mathias Rust's Cessna flight from Finland right into Red Square, penetrating Soviet air defences would have been no easy task. Major targets are ringed with modern phased array radars and new high-performance missiles, while the Soviets also retain vast numbers of older systems, such as the SA-2 'Guideline' seen here. It was an SA-2 that in 1960 brought down the U-2 piloted by Gary Powers, and so ushered in the age of low-level air warfare.

Right: The B-52's avionics are dedicated to countering enemy air defences. Behind the pilots, the defensive team of gunner and electronic warfare officer face to the rear, while beneath the flight deck the offensive team of navigator and radar navigator/bombardier inhabit their own red-lit world.

Below: The B-52's 'office' is dominated by the the cluster of engine dials and the huge bunch of throttle controls. Both flight crew have EVS screens. The aircraft commander, in the left-hand seat, has most of the secondary flight instrumentation, while the co-pilot has most of the comms controls.

Right: The electro-optical viewing system (EVS) gathers information via two rotating chin turrets. Behind the square window beneath the left-hand side of the nose is a low-light TV (LLTV) camera, while a forward-looking infra-red (FLIR) system looks through the oval window on the right.

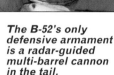

The B-52's only defensive armament is a radar-guided multi-barrel cannon in the tail.

5 Bomb run

Boeing's Offensive Avionics System includes a highly accurate inertial navigation system, plus terrain avoidance radar, computerised bombing systems, and a sophisticated electro-optical visual system (EVS). The navigation system gets the plane to the Initial Point (IP) of the bomb-run, and the pilot flies along a programmed track until weapon release. On a nuclear bomb run, the windscreen is covered with an aluminised anti-flash curtain, and the pilot uses the EVS for forward visibility. The EVS displays the output from the terrain avoidance radar together with a simplified reference line. The pilot must keep the reference line above the terrain trace, where in other terrain-following systems a computer does the job. The EVS also displays airspeed, altitude, a steering marker that indicates deviation from the correct bombing track, and time-to-weapon release.

6 Weapon release

When your weapons are missiles, fired hundreds or even thousands of kilometres from the target, it is vital to release them at the correct point. The B-52 can do this automatically. Information from the aircraft's inertial navigation systems and terrain contour-matching radar is compared with the data held on the mission tapes in the computerised Offensive Avionics System. As long as the bomber is in the right place, the electronics will ensure that the missiles are launched correctly.

Above: An AGM-86B air-launched cruise missile drops from the bomb bay of a Boeing B-52. The massive bomber can carry up to 18 of these accurate weapons, each with a warhead 10 times more powerful than the Hiroshima bomb.

Below: If a B-52 crew ever saw a sight like this, it might indicate a successful mission, but it would also mean that deterrence had failed and the world was coming to an end. It is to be hoped that it never happens.

The bomber's eyes

The Head Down Display, visible as blue screens in the cockpit photograph opposite, is a vital part of the B-52's offensive avionics system, The Electro-optical Vision System presents the flight crew with a picture from the chin-mounted LLTV (low-light TV) and FLIR (forward-looking infra-red) turrets. This is essential on an attack run, as direct vision is impossible since the cockpit windows are covered with aluminised anti-flash curtains. In addition, the head down display also gives rudimentary flight information: clockwise from the top left it indicates airspeed in knots; time to weapons release with heading reference markers beneath (line them up and you are on course); a vertical bar shows altitude in hundreds of feet; and at the bottom and at the left of the screen markers show the angle left or right and up and down in which the turret-mounted sensors are pointing. In the centre of the screen, a terrain avoidance horizontal reference line shows the path of the aircraft. If it is above the trace taken from the terrain avoidance radar, you are doing fine. If it is below, you are going to find yourself trying to fly through solid ground unless you pull up pretty quickly.

OPERATION BLACK BUCK

Operation Black Buck – the bombing of Port Stanley – was the longest bombing mission in history, and the first and only operational use of the massive Vulcan bomber.

It wasn't long before the Argentines knew that Britain meant business in the Falklands. But before Britain could launch its offensive, it would have to deal with the Argentine air force. If it could be restricted to the Argentine mainland, the British landings would take place at the very limit of enemy aircraft range.

Crews on the Black Buck mission take in the briefing before launching the longest and most complex single bombing raid in history.

To stop the Argentines using the paved runway at Port Stanley on the Falklands, the runway would have to be made unserviceable. That job was given to the Royal Air Force. But its nearest base was Wideawake Airfield on Ascension Island, some 4,000 miles away to the north of the Falklands. It would involve mounting the longest bombing raid in history.

Starting at 10.50 p.m. Ascension time (7.50 p.m. Stanley time) on 30 April, 11 supporting Victor tankers roared off the ground, closely followed by two Vulcans. Operation Black Buck was under way.

One Victor and one Vulcan were reserves, and it immediately became clear that both would be needed. One Victor could not wind out its refuelling hose, and the cabin of the primary Vulcan could not be pressurised.

The first transfer of fuel took place about one and three-quarter hours after take-off. Even during refuelling a problem manifested itself that was to become cumulatively greater with each hour that passed, and would finally jeopardise the success of the entire mission; for various reasons, the force was burning fuel at a far greater rate than had been envisaged.

"We had been told to leave the tankers with full tanks. I didn't have them, so I knew I was perfectly entitled to abort the mission," recalls the captain, Flight Lieutenant Withers, "but I thought that it was more

An ageing Vulcan is readied for the mission at Wideawake airfield, Ascension Islands. The aircraft type had virtually been retired after 27 years since its first flight. Only at this eleventh hour was it to drop bombs in anger.

Once a bomber like the Vulcan, a Victor tanker comes into land after a refuelling sortie. It would take 11 of these aircraft to keep one Vulcan fuelled for the 8,000-mile round trip to bomb Port Stanley airfield.

Above: A Vulcan's-eye view of a Victor tanker as it is about to take on the vital fuel load on its way to target. There were six such refuelling points and any one failure could mean the abandonment of the mission.

important to hit the target than to get the aircraft back. My priority was definitely to hit the target – and if we ended up in the drink that was tough.

"We approached the island more or less on heading and began let-down at about 290 miles. We did an airbrakeless descent of 1,500 to 2,500 feet per minute, 300 knots, throttles closed. We levelled out at 2,000 feet at about 230 miles. We had air speed indicator failure during the descent, which added to the excitement. We gradually stepped the descent down, eventually getting down to 300 feet at about 46 miles from the target. At 46 miles we pulled up to 500 feet to see if we could see anything on the radar, and as soon as we did the passive warning receiver came alive."

The receiver started to give out a short, high-pitched tone at 10-second intervals; it was picking up signals from the American-built TPS-43 early warning radar at Port Stanley, its scanner rotating at six revolutions per minute. Flight Lieutenant Withers continues:

"I was listening, but then I turned it off. At 34 miles we began our climb to 10,000 feet to give the bombs sufficient velocity to penetrate the runway before they went off. The island was just discernable through the gaps in the clouds. But I had my visors down as I was worried about loss of night vision from the flak I expected to come up. I really expected it to be like November 5th when the Argies opened up. I concentrated on flying straight and level, holding the correct attitude while our navigator confirmed that everything looked good. The offset points in the target area were showing.

"It was a smooth night; everything was steady. The range was coming down nicely. All of the switching had been made. We opened the bomb doors at about 11.5 miles from the target. I was expecting flak and perhaps missiles to come up, but nothing happened."

In fact, as the bomb doors opened the air electronics officer heard a distinctive high-pitched scratching note from his radar warning receiver as a Skyguard fire-control radar tried to lock on to the bomber. Skyguard was linked to 35-mm Oerlikon anti-aircraft guns whose shells might, at a pinch, reach the Vulcan's altitude. The AEO pushed the button on his control panel to activate the ALQ-101 jamming pod

Right: An aerial photo shows the bomb craters straddling the runway at Port Stanley. The string of bombs neatly crosses the runway and cuts the length in half, making it operationally useless for any combat aircraft.

Below: The Vulcan comes in to land at the end of its epic 16-hour mission.

Flight Lieutenant Withers is greeted after landing safely. It had been a tiring sortie, but his crew had dealt a serious blow to the Argentine forces.

under the starboard wing, and almost at once the enemy radar signals ceased.

As they approached Port Stanley under the electronic blanket the defending Argentine forces were unaware of the huge Vulcan above them until too late. As Flight Lieutenant Withers made his approach he released his entire bomb load of 21 1,000-lb bombs. "I had planned it that as soon as the bombs had gone, the throttles would go to the wall and we would do a 1.8-g full power climbing turn to the left. So I went into that, but since nothing was happening I eased off. It was a bit of an anti-climax.

"Forward throw was about two miles, from two miles up and flying at 350 knots. It was about

20 seconds from bomb release to the first bomb impacting; it took five seconds for all 21 bombs to go. At the time the first bombs exploded we were 15 seconds into our roll, having turned 45 degrees to port."

Because there has been some controversy about the attack, it should be pointed out that Withers was carrying out a textbook cutting operation. Certainly the operation could have been more effectively carried out using new systems such as the Tornado armed with JP 233 munitions, but not at this distance from base. The Vulcan's radar and general-purpose bombs represented 1940s technology, while the attack system dated back to the 1950s. Taking into account the known

inaccuracies of the Vulcan's various systems, the best chance of hitting the runway was to fly across it at an angle of 30 degrees and release the 21 bombs in a line at quarter-second intervals (50 ft).

In the co-pilot's seat, Pete Taylor glanced over to his left. Suddenly the clouds over the airfield were lit up from below. It was as if someone had switched on a bright but flickering light from behind a window of translucent glass. Then the darkness returned and the crew felt, rather than heard, the distant crump of the explosions merging together.

"After the attack the crew was very quiet, rather sad. We had just started a shooting war. It had been rather cold-blooded,

creeping in there at 4.30 in the morning to drop bombs on the place."

As the bomber clawed its way back to altitude, where each pound of fuel would take the machine twice as far as it would low down, Hugh Prior, the AEO, prepared the post-attack signal. Everyone in the crew agreed that the mission appeared to have been successful, so the code word "Superfuse" was transmitted.

"After that, the four hours back to Ascension were a bit of a bore," Withers remembers. "They seemed to last for ever." Nevertheless the Vulcan landed safely at Wideawake, after 16 hours in the air and having completed the longest bombing mission in history.